Mina Blair

Born in Oslo to a Norwegian mother and an American father, Mina now lives overlooking the inspiring Sussex Downs where she teaches online Hatha Yoga. Along with the regular classes, she offers MatChat™ Yoga, a bespoke practice working with the chakra subtle energy system to free up the body and mind from emotional burdens. She also publishes MatChat™ Podcasts where she talks to interesting people about all aspects of wellbeing – physical, mental, emotional and spiritual.

When not writing, teaching or broadcasting, Mina enjoys walking in the surrounding countryside with Barley, her constant canine companion.

Not for the last time is her first book.

Not for the last time

Mina Blair

For Francesca
The greatest spiritual teacher of all

Content

Introduction

The Bhagavad Gita

Acknowledgements

Mina's reading

Introduction

My life can be divided into three parts: Before Francesca, During Francesca and After Francesca.

I find it hard to remember who I was before she was born. That is another book. In retrospect, the twelve extraordinary years she was with us passed by quickly, and I'm not really sure how I got through that time. But what I do know is what happened to me after she left us, over the course of the twelve years that followed. A transformation I never thought possible in anyone, let alone myself. This is the story of *After Francesca*.

I dedicate this book to those who have suffered or are suffering but don't know why. It's not meant to be a prescriptive "how to…" guide, but rather a sharing of life experience that may offer understanding and clarity to others facing what seem like insurmountable challenges. It's my offering to the school of life. Because although life can be really tough, it is also a gift and a wonder, something that is easily forgotten in our constant striving for more than we already have.

The Bhagavad Gita

The Bhagavad Gita, which means "the song of the Lord", is one of the key ancient yogic Indian texts and of huge spiritual importance. It's a kind of map and guide book on how to find out who you really are and how to live a fulfilled life, including advice on choosing healthy food and having the right attitude towards self-discipline, giving, renunciation, work, happiness and more.

It was written around 500-400 BCE and appears in the sixth book of a huge epic called *The Mahabharata*, a story of struggle between two rival branches of the same family dynasty. *The Bhagavad Gita* story takes place just before a major battle is about to commence and the lead warrior on one side, called Arjuna, suddenly questions the purpose of it all. He has qualms about all the killing that will take place, about whether it's right to fight. His spiritual guide appears in the form of his charioteer, Sri Krishna, and the whole book is their conversation. It's a dialogue about the essentials of life and death. At the end, Arjuna can make what he feels is the right decision.

Of all the texts on spirituality that I have read, this remains for me the key. The one I keep coming back to over and over again because of its ongoing relevance to modern living and the human condition. It has been translated and interpreted by many authors, but I love Eknath Easwaran's treatment of this ancient story; he writes with such warmth, authenticity and clarity.

The verses that head up the chapters in this book are from his translation, *The Bhagavad Gita.* I chose each verse to reflect the sentiment, the message, of that particular chapter, and in that way, I'd like to think I'm linking the story of Arjuna to my own. If you are interested in reading Easwaran's book in full, it's worth reading his thoughts on its deeper meaning in *The Essence of The Bhagavad Gita* beforehand.

*Some come to the spiritual life because of
suffering, some in order to understand life;
some come through a desire to achieve life's
purpose, and some come who are
men and women of wisdom.
Bhagavad Gita 7.16*

Chapter 1: An ending and a beginning

"Wow, that was some night, whew!" she said,
slightly laughing.

Francesca and I were sitting on her hospital bed
in the paediatric ward of the regional hospital on
that Monday in late November 2007. We had been
there since she collapsed on Saturday evening, and
I had spent the two nights with her there. It was two
nights of many that we had passed in various
hospitals during her twelve years dealing with
various health crises. But that Sunday night was our
last.

Given the eventful night, Francesca was quite
calm, serene actually. She was wearing her pink
pyjamas with the smiling monkey faces on it, and if
it weren't for the clinical surroundings, you
wouldn't have sensed the recent drama. It had been
her second collapse since the first one six months

earlier, battling with deteriorating lungs caused by intra-uterine varicella syndrome. Put simply, I contracted chickenpox in the first trimester of pregnancy but rather than abort naturally, which would normally have happened, the foetus survived and Francesca was born with multiple issues where the virus had attacked the cells. We had found a way around most of them, from her club foot to the stenosis (narrowing) in her duodenum (small intestine), to the tracheostomy required to aid breathing (paralysed vocal chords partially blocking the airway), to the gastrostomy (tube into her stomach) required to bypass a faulty epiglottis that let food and liquid fall into her lungs. But the damage to the lungs already there at birth was irreparable. Fortunately, however, the virus had skipped her brain and she had developed into a funny, smart and charming little girl.

I had noticed a shift in Francesca's health at the beginning of that year; I could see she had stopped growing and breathing was becoming more challenging. The use of antibiotics and steroids had increased. I believe mothers have a special sense with their children, and I felt time was running out. Her zest for life had inspired us all over the years, in spite of the pain she suffered and being "stuck in this wonky body" as she would say when going through a rough patch. A loving light emanated from her 24/7, constantly reminding us to appreciate and enjoy the little things, things you would probably miss in a busy daily routine. Like noticing a red kite, her favourite bird, flying overhead, or finding a pretty meadow flower and poring over it, looking at the details. She loved her food, always wanting to know what we were having days in advance so she could look forward to it (we had eventually been able to remove the feeding tube).

But the journey was drawing to a close. As Francesca pointed out, that Sunday night had indeed been a wild ride. She had been put on strong intravenous antibiotics that had basically had a hallucinogenic effect, giving her disturbing dreams. It had also made her need to urinate every two hours, a project involving bringing all the intravenous kit with us to and from the toilet. I carried her in one arm and rolled the IV stand on wheels with the other. We inevitably got a bit tangled, resulting in laughs and giggles, but also continuous apologies from her as we juggled our way back and forth. She could see I was tired.

"I'm so sorry, Momsie, I need to go wee again!"

"It's all right, Nut, don't worry, just let me get sorted with all this stuff and we'll be on our way." Nut, short for Nutkin, had been her nickname since she was a toddler – she had loved the Beatrix Potter story of Squirrel Nutkin and it just, well, stuck somehow. Francesca was very small due to the lung disease that affected her breathing capacity, so having a nickname implying something small in size felt appropriate.

There had been a steady build-up of fluid in her lungs throughout the night as well, and we had to send for the night nurse to do some deep suctioning. The nurse in charge turned out to be an attractive young man, which did not go unnoticed by

Francesca. The procedure itself was very unpleasant, involving passing a plastic tube right down into the bronchial branch and then suctioning. The noise of the machine with the accompanying coughing and gagging was disturbing, to say the least, but Francesca took it in her usual brave stride, and it gave her some short relief.

After he left the first time she immediately looked at me and said, "He's very handsome, that was lucky!" and we had a little giggle.

After the second suctioning, it was decided that that was enough, the lung tissue would just become more inflamed, and the fluid build-up was not abating in any case. The doctor on duty came to take her bloods and came back distressed with the news that the blood gases were rising. It is a fact that when lung function deteriorates, the CO_2 level rises in the bloodstream, since you can't balance it with the inhaled oxygen. With less and less oxygen going in, death is inevitable. I could tell from his agitation he was new to the dying child scenario, poor guy. I remained calm.

"So, the story ends here and in this way," I thought. It was such a strange feeling, strangely comforting. I had spent the last 12 years knowing Francesca would not reach adulthood but not knowing how and when it would end. It's a mother's instinct, you see, mothers just *know*. I had developed a fear of not being there, of somehow missing her last hours. I had put her into this world and I needed to see her out.

And so there we were, alone in her hospital room enjoying some peace and quiet now that all the bleeping machinery had been removed. The circus had left town, as it were, and we were able to just be still for a while. I had spoken with the doctors and agreed to end treatment, the plan being to get Francesca home as soon as possible so she could die there, surrounded by her family and her beloved cat, in the home she loved so much. Concerned we would run out of time and desperate for her not to die in hospital, I asked for the leaving process to be organised as quickly as possible. They went off to put into action the administrative process of a final patient discharge. In a few moments I was going to call Francesca's father, Malcolm, and tell him where we had got to overnight and the plan to come home. He would need to contact the school where our older daughter, Karina, was and collect her so they could meet us in hospital. We would leave the hospital together.

For now, it was just the two of us. I just had to be real with her, she deserved this much after all she had been through in her short life. Sitting on the side of the bed and holding her hand, I said, "Francesca, I am just so very sorry that I cannot think of anything more to do for you, to help you…" I started to cry and let the tears come. "If there was something, anything, I would do it, you know that. I love you so very much."

Her face was a picture of peace and knowing, she was relaxed.

"Don't worry, Momsie, you're the best mum in the world." Her tone was quite matter-of-fact. She was saying I hadn't needed to say it, she always knew how much she was loved.

I then told her that we were going home as soon as possible and her face lit up.

"But not for the last time," she said.

The inflection was somewhere between a question and a statement. Whether she was reassuring me or herself, or perhaps not wanting to acknowledge the ending, I don't know, but not wanting to upset or frighten her I said "no".

Calling Malcolm now was the hardest thing I had needed to do in all the past twelve years. We had been in phone touch every day about Francesca since forever, thousands of phone hours. But not this. There had been so many near-endings in Francesca's precarious life, and yet we always pulled through. With every passing birthday and Christmas she defied the odds. When she was born our family life came to a complete halt as we fought the regular life-threatening health fires until she approached two years old and a sort of stability had emerged. Up to that point I had resigned myself to losing her and was waiting for the moment to arrive. But it didn't, and life had to go on. Neither he nor I were earning at this time, and the financial situation was dire, so something had to change. Given the 27-year age gap between us, it was decided that I would look for full-time work as soon as possible and he would look after the two girls. It was not a willing choice I made – when we had got together and agreed to have children it was on the premise that I stayed at home – but we were playing a different game now and the goal posts had been moved significantly. It was simply about what needed to be done. I did get a job and financial security was restored.

The marriage had not survived, however; we had been divorced for nearly three years now. But we had remained close to share the child care, which is why I lived in town just minutes away. I had recently bought a house there with my new partner, Hamish, and together we worked as a team to support Francesca.

But here we were, at the end of the road. There was nothing else to pull out of the hat. I called and relayed the night's events and what the medical decision was, to take Francesca home and make her comfortable while she died. I think a sort of surreal incredulity comes over one in these sorts of extreme situations. It must be shock, but a matter-of-fact, get-organised mentality takes over, probably to prevent complete emotional collapse. I heard it in my voice and I heard it in his. He agreed to deal with the school, collect Karina and come to the hospital straight away. Time was of the essence since no one knew how quickly the blood gases would rise and I was terrified she would die before seeing them, let alone die in hospital.

The day unfolded in its weird way. We were reunited mid-morning, feeling happy that we could focus on the homecoming. We all stayed calm for Francesca, I felt very proud about that, and especially of her 15-year-old sister. The girls were very close and it had been a constant source of joy to me to see the deep love and connection that was expressed between them always. But getting a final medical sign-off is not done in minutes. Malcolm and I had to attend a meeting with the doctors to discuss and agree officially Francesca's assisted death at home. Paperwork had to be produced and signed. We were provided with a sedative to give her when she was put to bed for the night, to make sure she was comfortable. We had to transport her in an ambulance, which had to be booked and waited for.

It was all I could do to not lose my composure completely as the hours passed and the afternoon wore on. I felt such an intense sense of urgency, she simply couldn't die in hospital. I sensed Francesca holding out, however; she was excited to get home too. In the usual manner, we agreed in advance what she was having for dinner – her favourite, pasta with tomato sauce drizzled with olive oil.

It was the delay of the ambulance arriving that turned out to be the hold-up, but finally, at half past five, Francesca and I set off on our last journey. We had been here before many times, rushed off to hospital in an ambulance for various emergencies, more often when she was little and then less as she got older. It's strange to say it, but my overwhelming feeling at this point was relief. Francesca was safe, she would have the peaceful, calm and dignified death she deserved, with her beloved family around her. The ending would be on our terms. She would suffer no more pain, no more dread for the needles that always came whenever we had to go to hospital.

She was wrapped up on a stretcher and I was in a seat next to her.

"So, Nut, we're off home at last!" I said cheerfully, wanting to remain light and positive.

She looked up at me, smiling, "But not for the last time."

There it was again. She was so calm and I sensed no fear in her. At no point during the day had we explicitly said she was soon going to die, but Francesca had always had a sixth sense, a kind of *knowing*. Like the first time she had said these words, I wasn't sure whether she was reassuring me or herself, so again I said "no".

Father and sister were already at the house when we arrived, with Hamish joining us minutes later. As we busied ourselves preparing dinner you would have thought it was just any other normal day really. Francesca was so joyful, cuddling the cat and anticipating the pasta. As a special treat, though, she was allowed to eat in her bedroom while watching her favourite programme *Eastenders* on TV. Her sister and cat joined her, all piled up on the bed. While the girls were upstairs sharing this precious time together, the grown-ups ate downstairs, chatting about this and that. The atmosphere was one of love and calm, we just all naturally and instinctively felt this was what the situation required.

With dinner done, I helped get Francesca ready for bed. Hamish said his goodbyes to her and went back to our house. She was given the sedative and tucked up in bed as normal, each of us giving goodnight kisses and cuddles in the usual way. She soon fell asleep. The three of us now had to discuss how we wanted to manage the night. There was no knowing when the final moment would arrive, it could be into the next morning. To check Francesca's oxygen blood levels we had always had a saturation monitor at home, so we connected that to her finger as she slept, as an indicator of how she was doing. Karina decided she didn't want to be present when Francesca passed, so she would go to bed and be left until the morning. Having been up for the last two nights in hospital, I was too exhausted to stay awake throughout a third, so we agreed that Malcolm would keep watch and wake me up in the spare room when the saturation monitor showed we were close to the end. By this time, we had moved Francesca to the main bedroom to have more space and be able to lie next to her.

So we settled down for the night, there was nothing else to do, nothing else to be said. Perhaps we were still functioning in that incredulous state from the morning when we realised where we had got to as a family, I don't know. Perhaps we were overwhelmed with the reality, the finality. I mean, is there a right way to say your final, conscious goodbye to your child or sister? A right way to behave? We all expressed our deep love for her in the goodnights, and she for us, there was nothing left unsaid for any of us. That seemed enough.

I can't say I slept properly, more that I faded in and out until I got the signal that we needed to gather. It was just gone 4.00 am. Francesca was clearly in a deep slumber but the monitor showed the oxygen level was low. It wouldn't be long now, so we unhooked the machine. I lay beside her on the bed and remembered that hearing is the last sense we lose when we die, so I whispered in her ear repeatedly how much I loved her and that it would be all right, to not be afraid, we were all there.

Suddenly Karina appeared at the door with the cat at her feet. It gave me a start and I asked if she was all right, given she had said she wanted to sleep undisturbed.

"I was woken up by the cat, she jumped up on my chest just now!"

"Gosh, how strange. Francesca is about to go, sweetheart, do you want to stay with us?"

Yes, the cat clearly wanted her to be there and she chose to stay. I quietly thought that Francesca had got the cat to wake her, wanting us to share her passing together. And so we gathered round in the quiet of the night. No more bleeping machines or hissing nebulisers. Francesca's naturally noisy breathing became gradually slower until, just after five, she let out one final, long exhale and we were enveloped in complete silence for the first time in twelve years. It was deafening.

Time and space seemed to vanish. In that last exhale I felt something extraordinary, that her spirit left her body and hovered around us, resting above the scene. I had a clear vision from above, as if looking down from the ceiling at the three of us and the cat huddled around her body. As if she was taking us in for the last time in this world. And then she was gone.

The tears could now come, the pent-up emotion held on to all day and night was released. Twelve years of an unbelievable life for us all, an extraordinary existence, was over. The world as we knew it had come to an end and yet a new day dawned on our, now smaller, family. Surprisingly for me, the sun rose up and somehow I had to get on. The first thing to be done was to call the GP and inform him of Francesca's passing. He had been informed of our situation the day before and I had been given his mobile number for this moment. Again, how do you speak and function when your heart has been completely shattered? I don't know but something else takes over. Not long after, he arrived to perform the formality of declaring her dead. Another surreal moment. He said he would organise for the hearse to come and collect her body.

A hearse? A word that had not entered my vocabulary before. And I had not considered all this, the *after*. My whole focus had been on the ending, not on the inevitability of what would follow. I now realised I would need to let go of Francesca physically, to part with her physical presence. I felt very strongly that it had to be me who would carry her body out of the house. I could not allow anyone else to do it. Needing to be close to her for a bit longer, though, I laid next to her body, just taking it all in, all the details. The softness of her fine hair, the long eyelashes, the delicate hands. I didn't want to ever forget the *feel* of her.

When the hearse arrived, the moment could not be put off any longer. I wrapped her in her favourite blanket and carried her out of the house and down to the vehicle. She was surprisingly heavy. It was all so very still, the air, the countryside. As if a collective breath was being held. And as the hearse drove away, leaving me emptyhanded physically and emotionally, my heart shattered a bit more.

One doesn't appreciate all the practicalities of death in the first instance. You have just lost someone special and ought to work with that. Instead, it's paperwork, phone calls, meetings. Just more of the surreal, to be honest.

There was a lot to decide about the funeral. Not being churchgoers, I had assumed that a burial was not possible, not allowed. We decided to spread her ashes along the Sussex Downs just above the house which she loved so much, and where she had spent a lot of time enjoying the flora and fauna on the countless picnics there. However, this bothered me hugely because of a random conversation I had had with the girls about a year before. I can't remember how we got onto the subject (yet strangely telling), but one way or another we were discussing how we felt about cremation and burial. Francesca was adamant that being buried was better – the thought of being burned to a crisp terrified her. Interestingly, her sister felt the opposite; she was appalled by the thought of her body rotting underground in the dark. We had a laugh about it. But I knew our chat was important and filed it somewhere in the back of my mind.

Then, as if sent by Francesca herself, the village vicar called in. Colin had heard of Francesca's death and came to see how we were and to offer support. He felt strongly that she should have a grave, a place of connection where the family could go to grieve.

What were our thoughts on that? When I shared what Francesca had said about her preference for a burial, the matter was settled immediately. He said we could go to the churchyard and choose a lovely spot with a view towards the Downs. I can't put into words how grateful and relieved I was. The thought of sending her into the flames that frightened her and going against her wishes had tormented me until that moment. When we went to look, it was obvious where she should go. Under a tree next to a bench, where we could sit whenever we felt like it and, well, be, I guess.

Colin turned out to be a godsend in the truest sense of the word. With his guidance we managed to organise a fitting service that everyone was comfortable with. We also wanted to be as inclusive as possible, to involve Francesca's friends if they wished. One of the hardest things was to inform the school of her death. Although Francesca had been too ill to attend school regularly during her life – she was mostly home-schooled – she always enjoyed going and being with children her own age. She had managed to make a few friends there. The deputy head, who had been very supportive of Francesca's school life and was clearly upset with the news, held a special assembly to inform the teachers and students, then gathered her friends to discuss the funeral. I was deeply touched when I heard they all wanted to not only attend, but to stand up as a group and pay tribute to Francesca as part of the service. I thought this brave, being themselves only twelve years old.

Again, I think I managed the whole funeral preparation from a place of numbness. I just wanted it over with so I could be alone with my grief, alone to have some space. But details had to be decided on: what she would wear in the coffin (a favourite party dress), the design and content of the funeral service programme, the music, the photograph, where to go after the service and booking that, ordering the food. I particularly struggled with what to wear. I mean, how do you choose the outfit for your child's funeral? Is there a "right" look? In the end I opted for a charcoal grey woollen dress with a white collared shirt underneath. Funereal enough yet practical. I'm not sure Francesca would have approved actually, she loved colour (pink and purple her favourites) and always wore bright clothes.

There was one thing I just couldn't do, though, and that was to see her body in the funeral home. I didn't want my last image of her to be in some strange, unfamiliar and emotionally cold place. Also, I just don't think my heart could have managed another parting after carrying her out of the house the day she died. Instead, I dropped off the pearl necklace I wanted her to wear, a present I had given her years before.

The day of the funeral dawned grey and wet, typical of an English December. I just wanted it done, frankly. I was exhausted from the sheer effort of basic functioning along with all the conversations with people and managing their feelings. I was staggered by some reactions, in particular one person responding with "you must be relieved". If it was meant to be supportive and helpful, I didn't feel it. It's strange, but even after years of caring for someone with disability, one's reaction on losing that person is not to rush out and book that family holiday abroad you always wanted to go on but couldn't. There is simply this now-empty space that really, really hurts. Others couldn't face coming to the funeral and made their excuses.

The level of surrealness sky-rocketed as I stood on the first row of the pews in front of the church and heard Francesca's coffin being carried towards me. A quick sideways glance and I could see it resting on a wooden frame, her portrait photograph standing next to it on an easel. Clutching the programme, I hung on to the order of service as it moved through its various parts, the hymns, the vicar's sermon. Francesca's friends had decided to present an acrostic poem they had made, describing what they liked about her. It was hard for them but I was grateful for their courage, Francesca would have loved it.

I couldn't speak at all. With the service finished we followed the coffin out to the graveyard to the chosen spot, where the hole had been dug in readiness. With everyone gathered around, the coffin was lowered into the ground, the final leg of Francesca's incredible journey. As I tossed my symbolic fistful of earth on top of the coffin I was overcome with the urge to jump into the grave and be buried with her, to shout and wail, to pull my hair out and beat my chest. Not to stand there motionless, quietly crying.

I later reflected on the more expressive and open funeral rites of other cultures where one can wail and show grief collectively, thinking how much more appropriate and natural that is. And not be expected to "manage". It got worse after the funeral as we went to the local pub for lunch. Here I found myself playing "the hostess with the most-ess", doing the rounds and talking to the guests, chatting and making small talk to make it easier for them and having some laughs. Because what do you talk about with someone who has just buried their child? It is just too awkward in our culture, sadly. I was concerned about how Karina would cope, but when I saw her she was completely surrounded by her gorgeous friends, sitting on their laps, being hugged and stroked. Thank God for that, young people able to connect instinctively to what was needed and express themselves freely.

It was kind of the lead paediatric medical doctor from the local hospital to make the time to attend the funeral. We had a brief but revealing conversation in the pub. In the summer when Francesca had had her first collapse and went to hospital, we asked Francesca if she would like to talk to this doctor herself in private. We had always encouraged her to feel ownership of her body and not talk past her in the room. After all, she was the one who had to go through all the treatments and the pain, so the least we could do was to respect her as an individual in this way. And sometimes there are things that are easier to say to a third party than to your family. In any case, Francesca accepted the offer and talked to the doctor alone. He now told me what she had said.

"We chatted about this and that for a while, but when I moved onto the subject of managing her health in future, she just smiled at me and quite calmly said she would not be alive at Christmas."

Yes, I was not at all surprised to hear that. Francesca had always had a sixth sense, as I said, but I think we have this ability to tune in and sense the ending in cases of illness. It certainly explained her urgency in discussing with me what she wanted to give as Christmas presents, not necessary in early November. She was adamant I write a list and we went out to buy the gifts. When it was all done and organised, her sense of relief and satisfaction was clear but I didn't dwell on the significance of it. I probably knew what it meant but couldn't fully go there yet.

And then the day was over.

What do I do now? Where do I go from here?

The offering of wisdom is better than any material
offering... for the goal of all work is
spiritual freedom.
Bhagavad Gita 4.33

Chapter 2: Coffee and cats

In September the following year a letter from the vicar arrived addressed to me. It was a thank you letter in response to the donation we had made to the church as a gesture of our sincere gratitude. I had expressed how much I appreciated the way Colin supported us in organising the funeral and the grave. The gravestone had just recently been put in place and he liked the inscription we had chosen underneath Francesca's name and the date of her death: *Small body - big heart - great smile.*

The previous nine months of my life had passed in a kind of haze. I had been allowed one month off work, and before I knew it I was back to commuting to and from London in my usual corporate role. I tried to "click back in", being as normal as I could to make things easier for the people at the office. The effort was exhausting. Yet I couldn't distract myself from the thoughts that tormented me night and day. I had descended helplessly and uncontrollably into an existential, spiritual crisis. I was having regular panic attacks and moments of feeling overwhelmed with dread, which sat heavy in the pit of my stomach like a hard, cold lump of metal that wouldn't go away.

I wasn't a religious person and had no such framework or base to fall back on to help work through my grief. My single parent background was devoid of anything spiritual, my mother being an ardent, aggressive atheist who often refused to set foot in a church, even for concerts or to admire the architecture and the artwork. Suddenly my daughter was gone and I just couldn't understand it. I was left with a multitude of seemingly unanswerable questions. What the hell had just happened? Why did it have to happen? Why me? Why her? Where did she go? Where do we all go? Is there something more after death or just, well, nothing? What are we here for, if anything? And so on. I needed to do something, I couldn't just leave her behind me in the past, like some random, one-off unlucky event. A dark secret. Her life couldn't have meant *nothing*. I needed to find *meaning*. Otherwise, how could I get on with my life?

Unbelievably, I had got through that first Christmas and New Year. I didn't know I had so many tears to cry. Yet the world kept turning, the days turned into weeks, weeks into months, but those key questions wouldn't stop swirling around in my head. Rather than settling down I became more agitated. So, when I read his letter I reflected once more on the kindness and understanding Colin had shown in our time of crisis. In it he wrote:

I am heartened to know I was of some help to you in such a painful time. If I can help again do not hesitate to get in touch with me.

Of course, Francesca will always be part of your life and even if, as I hope, the pain of loss will lessen, she will always live in your heart as I believe she also lives in God.

I noted the reference to God but didn't feel put off by it. It didn't feel as if it was meant in a religious way. I wondered whether I could share my thoughts with him. Perhaps I should take him up on his offer? He didn't seem to be the classic judgemental fire-and-brimstone take-the-bible-literally type of religious representative. "It's God's will" was simply not going to cut it for me. I decided to take a chance and write him a reply. I didn't waste any ink and cut straight to the chase already in the second sentence:

I wanted to write back to you because I have been in some considerable pain and turmoil this year trying to reconcile myself and my beliefs over the question of where Francesca has gone and whether I shall ever be with her again (in any form). I have also been rather distressed about a particular issue that happened the night she died, so I will tell you about that first.

I proceeded to explain that while I was next door resting, with Malcolm keeping an eye on the saturation monitor with orders to alert me when the end neared, she had suddenly woken up out of her drug-induced slumber. This was not meant to happen, obviously. She had needed to go to the toilet and he had taken her to the bathroom. While there, she had asked him quite calmly and lucidly, "When am I going to die, Pappa?" He had replied "when you're ready". She had then said she was sorry, presumably meaning sorry that she was dying and leaving us. He reassured her everything would be okay and tucked her back up in bed after giving her some more sedative.

He told me about this exchange when I came back into the bedroom just before she died. I had since been plagued with the idea that her last thought of me was that I wasn't present, that mum was away as usual at work or at her house. I had not been able to shake this intense guilt.

I then went on in the letter to talk about some reading I had done. The bereavement counsellor I had been seeing mentioned the work of Dr Elisabeth Kubler-Ross, a book called *On Children and Death*. This doctor had spent most of her working life with terminally ill patients, especially children. During this time she also gathered a significant number of near-death cases. The way she described people close to death and then dying was exactly the way Francesca had been. Peace and serenity take over the person, complete calm, and the person knows and accepts he/she is dying. Then when the body ceases to function, the spirit (or whatever you want to call it) passes out of the body on the last long exhale and at that moment the person can "see" where they are, the people who are there, before going into a bright light to be embraced by people who preceded them and loved them. Near-death cases, regardless of location in the world or religious/cultural background, all describe this same thing: reuniting with loved ones, a feeling of all-encompassing peace and love, and also, especially for those who were sick or injured, a feeling of having a whole and normal body.

As described in the previous chapter, I actually experienced this myself in the moment of her passing, the exiting of Francesca's spirit and it hovering momentarily. Reading the Kubler-Ross book not only reassured me that Francesca had had a peaceful, indeed, beautiful death, but it helped me begin to understand the existence of this other "place". That we don't enter some black void and that's the end of it, but rather we go somewhere. Maybe *dimension* is the right word.

In any case, I finished the letter with:

It is very painful still to have one beloved child in each world, so to speak. Each day I want to go to one and yet stay with the other. This bright light and embracing love is of course what you call God, and others call whatever their religious belief dictates. For me it doesn't matter because we will all pass over, and so personally, I would describe myself as spiritual. In other words, I believe in the essence/spirit of religion, but not when taken in the literal sense. Meanwhile, I shall try to make the most of my time in the physical time-and-space.

And I just wanted you to know that I now understand what you mean when you say Francesca will always live in my heart and that she lives with God. I believe that is where she is, too.

It was important to me that Colin understood right up front the non-religious nature of my spiritual quest, that I was not looking to be converted or anything like that. I had to be honest about that if he was going to help me.

Two weeks later I was delighted to receive another letter. I took it as a sign we could begin to share some ideas. In it, he put religion into a broader context, and I include the full contents here:

An image some people find helpful when thinking about the best in some religious traditions is that of a wheel: we all start either from the rim or a little way down one of the spokes; all the spokes lead down to the centre, converging as they go; the centre is the ultimate truth or the love at the heart of all that exists. There is no neutral language which we can use to talk about the centre: Buddhists may speak of Nirvana, Christians of God, but, strikingly, both experience this centre as all-embracing compassionate love. We find their suffering and death painful; grief measures our love, even if at times we find some consolation. In time, the sharpness of grief usually becomes less acute.

Love is also the evidence that death is not the end. The compassionate love at the heart of all things, at the hub of the wheel, at the centre, is perfect. Those we love are also loved by this ultimate love, and by that love are held and perfected beyond the death which seems to separate them from us.

This image of the wheel may also suggest that existence is far greater than our own limited experience of it suggests. All of us may journey towards the great love at the heart of existence, some may progress further than others, for all sorts of reasons, but all of us are loved and what we glimpse in our lives is but a fragment of what will one day be fully revealed, at the centre.

The life we have in this world is part of a greater gift to come. Like all gifts, we should receive our life with gratitude and learn to use our lives as fully as opportunity offers us. All life is a precious gift, whether that life is short or long.

This may seem difficult, but the death of those we love does not mean the end of their living and loving, their love for us, ours for them. Also, such deaths should not make us value less the gift of life which we have: those who love us would not wish it so.

Your grief at Francesca's death has brought you into a place where darkness and light are both present. When there is light, try to see what is revealed; when it is dark, endure it as best you can until the next shaft of light enlightens you.

He then signed off, saying he was available for more letters, emails or a meeting to chat. Well, you can imagine the relief and joy at reading something that made sense to me, that was in tune with how I was *feeling*! And this first letter actually helped explain another issue I was grappling with. I had noticed that my love for Francesca remained just as strong, it was the same as when she was alive, which is why I hurt so much. I had the love to give but the recipient was gone. It just sat there in my heart, taking up the same space and going nowhere, aching. I hated it when people said, "Oh, at least you have Karina," as if that was some kind of compensation and would make the grief less. As if I could transfer the balance in the "Francesca love bank account" to the "Karina love bank account" and close it. So that *all* my love could now go to Karina and make up for (or mask even) the emptiness.

Love is non-transferable! Love is infinite! Of course it is, if you think about it. You're not given a love quota for life when you are born, to share amongst the people you care about. Then when a person leaves your life in whatever way you now get "spare love" to allocate to someone else. No, no, no. Grief is working with the love that remains for that person. That's the constant ache which is so painful. It's also the reason why telling a bereaved person that "at least you have [name of another child or beloved]" is absolutely **not** helpful.

In my letter back to Colin I shared these thoughts, but I also posed him a tricky question:

I understand what you say about God is love, but there is something that bothers me, and actually, what has alienated me from religion so far. That is the concept of Hell – sinners being defined by religion. It is so judgemental – it is saying that God does not love all, the "bad" people go to Hell. But if we all go to this place of love when we die, where does Hell fit in? This is why I have not believed in a "God", because I am against this idea of judgement and sentencing upon dying. Who decides? To some religious people I guess I may go there myself, depending on what the criteria are.

The reply was swift. I include it here verbatim because this was the point when I could "spiritually relax" into the exploration, as he put what was left of my anxiety and resistance to rest:

There are passages in the bible which suggest that God will judge us by our deeds, but in the Old Testament, the Hebrew scriptures, there is little of a concept of an afterlife. There are passages in the New Testament which speak of God's judgement at the end of time and, in that judgement, the ones who have not acted with compassion are sent to an eternal fire. From such passages the traditional and familiar picture of heaven and hell has been constructed. I have never believed it. The bible should be read intelligently, not literally.

What I do believe is that all creation at its heart is good. This is not to deny that there is suffering and evil marring the book of nature, the key is to read and understand the meaning of the book of nature. Just as with a book, it may have torn or stained pages, but what matters is the meaning we can learn from the sentences of the book. I believe that the meaning of the book of nature is that goodness, untarnished, untouched by evil is at its heart. This goodness is God's loving gift to us.

Since all of us are part of nature, each one of us is at heart good. Sometimes people do act unjustly, cruelly or selfishly, but their actions cannot destroy or corrupt the basic goodness of their natures, only obscure it from themselves and others.

There is no anger or judgementation in God, only loving goodness. The anger and judgementalism is entirely from us.

Well, there we are, I thought. This made sense. I could stop being so hung up on the word God being literal, you know, the guy with the long white beard deciding who is in and who is out. My spiritual and religious ignorance had kept me there, but now I could let that go and embrace the word God in a different way. I felt relieved, liberated even.

At the end of the letter Colin suggested I look at a couple of short books to help me form an alternative view, an ancient version of Christianity free from the wicked doctrine of God as The Judge and Consigner of Souls to Hell. These were J Philip Newell's *The Book of Creation* and *Celtic Benediction*. I ordered both immediately. In my letter back to Colin saying I had ordered the books and thanking him for the recommendation, I shared my final thoughts on life being judged:

...it makes me think that each person starts with love, and then from birth it is either nurtured and enhanced, or gradually destroyed. Therefore, it makes sense that when we die we go back to where we started, with love. It is depressing looking at all the cruelty and suffering in the world, created by man, when in the bigger scheme of things it is quite pointless.

I went through a phase after Francesca was born, and now again after she died, of thinking how unfair it was that a person as loved and loving as she, died, rather than someone else who would be better off "put out of their misery". But life of course is not like that, both loved and unloved children (and adults) die. There is no judgement, it just is what it is. Hence I could not relate to the concept of "God's will" – that Francesca's death was the result of a proactive divine act. But that is a literal interpretation again. I just don't like hearing people say it – it demeans all our efforts here on Earth, and worse, makes us unaccountable and irresponsible for things we say and do, and for things that happen. I feel it is an easy, convenient excuse.

I am musing that ancient peoples of the world would have known about near-death experiences, heard about the loving light, and hence traditional belief is related to that in some way. I hope so. Francesca certainly seemed to be connected to this Earth in a different way, it is hard to explain. I can only describe it as someone else did to me when they first met Francesca. They said it felt like she "has been here before", she seems "an older (ancient) person than her years". I am thinking maybe she was partly in the next dimension all along when she was alive. Several people, not related, remarked on this.

Colin opened the door of the vicarage with a welcoming smile and showed me through to the little kitchen at the back. It was the end of October and we had been corresponding through letters for a couple of months now. We had naturally fallen into a rhythm of me reading a chapter in *The Book of Creation* and then writing my thoughts on that chapter and sending it to him. He would then reply with his thoughts. We had so far covered three chapters in this way and I was enjoying it very much. This was our first meeting to discuss ideas further. Newell's book takes each day of Genesis in the bible as a chapter and offers a Celtic version, applying a sort of overlay of Celtic spirituality. This form of Christianity seemed to resonate with me. The main themes I was particularly drawn to were:

- The Christian premise that people are basically good and not sinners who need reining in
- The importance of the elements in connecting us to our spiritual inner self
- The complementary (symbiotic) relationship and equal importance of men and women
- The significance of birds in Celtic symbolism

The last point impacted me the most. Francesca had been a keen birdwatcher, probably because she spent most of her life in a house in the country, but also because she seemed naturally drawn to them. She knew the name of every bird that visited the garden and those she saw when taken on picnics and excursions up on the Downs. Her favourite was the Red Kite, a beautiful raptor that seemed able to soar continuously without ever having to flap its wings. The reference to the elements resonated also, connecting me to my childhood in Norway where we lived very much according to the rhythm of the seasons and close to nature. This was especially so at the cabin in the mountains which we visited during school holidays in winter and summer. We were never unaware of the elements there, put it that way. And the reference to the equality of men and women, so important to me. Again, maybe this touched my Scandinavian culture, but frankly, how else could it be? In nature, both male and female work together, procreating as they do to secure the survival of their species. Why couldn't humans do the same?

The cafetière was ready on the kitchen counter, waiting for hot water. There was a table tucked into the corner with two adjacent chairs where he gestured for me to sit. And then, what joy! Underneath the table was a blanket on top of which lay two beautiful Burmese cats. I fell to my knees instantly.

"Oh! Cats! I love cats!" I exclaimed as I reached out to stroke them. They were both friendly and responded enthusiastically to my fussing, pushing their faces hard into my hand. Their loud purring felt so soothing, their coats so silky soft. I don't know why, but interacting with felines always prompts me to speak my native Norwegian, it seems to happen automatically. This time was no exception. Intrigued, Colin turned around to look as he pushed the plunger down to make the coffee.

"Sorry about that, I can't help it! But did you know all cats understand Norwegian?"

"No, can't say I was aware of that. But they seem to, don't they?"

He brought the coffee and two mugs over to the table as I got up from the floor and sat down. To my delight, one of the cats jumped up and settled on my lap. "What are their names?" I asked.

"Ione and Petra. They are sisters."

"How lovely!"

The cats settled down as we started our discussion and went over what I had gleaned so far from the book. What I liked about Newell were his references to other spiritual sources. One of these was the poet Kenneth White and his collected works *The Bird Path*, which I had managed to purchase. At the front of this book it explained that "to tread the bird path" is a Chinese expression which means realising self-nature. He writes:

A flying bird leaves no tracks in the air, like the self-nature which leaves no traces anywhere, for it is omnipresent and beyond location and direction.

I had not thought about that before, birds flying leaving no trace but they were definitely there. It was consistent with the Celtic bird symbolism which I now understood to mean that, like a bird's flight, our spirit leaves no trace yet it is everywhere. It just can't be seen literally with our eyes. I felt Francesca was like a bird now – she had left her earthly shell but her trace was still there.

My favourite Kenneth White poem was *Walking the Coast* which had wonderful references to nature and the spiritual but was also my first introduction to the concept of the all-knowing-but-unknowable, the something-greater-than-myself. This poem is made up of no less than 53 parts or "bits", and Part 28 caught my attention in particular:

Knowing now
That the life
At which I aim
Is a circumference
Continually expanding
Through sympathy and
Understanding
Rather than an exclusive centre
Of pure self-feeling
The whole I seek
Is centre plus circumference
And now the struggle at the centre is over
The circumference beckons from everywhere.

Yes indeed, I had been struggling at the centre my whole life up to now, stuck in "self-feeling". Over coffee I shared this thought, that I had been stuck in fear, and therefore in anger, for so long. But I was ever so slowly and gradually beginning to let go of the fear. Fear of the not knowing, the fear of everything basically. I realised how this had completely shut down my creative energy, which was now making itself felt through the reading and letter writing. I was slowly waking up, opening my eyes and taking a look around me now that it was safe to do so with Colin as a guide. I could stop feeling alone. Newell had summarised in chapter three my current state of mind very aptly: *the fallow fields of our souls, that have been 'long left unploughed' need to be turned over.* Again, reference to nature and the elements, with beautiful imagery that I could see, feel and even smell.

"Well, I'm certainly starting to turn over my unploughed fields for sure," I remarked as I finished my coffee. It was time to go. I reluctantly placed the sleeping cat back on the floor. We agreed to continue the correspondence, taking the remaining four chapters of Newell's *Book of Creation* in turn, but meeting once more before Christmas.

As I walked out the door I thanked Colin for his time. "And I look forward to our next session of coffee and cats!"

"Me too, see you then."

During the weeks in between, I immersed myself in Newell as much as I could. I was working full time, commuting to and from London. I had got through Francesca's birthday followed by her death anniversary but Christmas loomed large. The letters kept me anchored. We covered chapters four through six which introduced the philosophic works of Pelagius and Eriugena. There was also an exchange on science vs spirituality, for example, pondering the question, how can you prove God exists or does not exist?

Pelagius sounded like a cool guy. He lived around 360-420 CE a British monk and theologian who was brave enough to push back on the powerful proclamations of (Saint) Augustine, another theologian and influential philosopher living in Roman North Africa at the same time. He did not buy Augustine's idea that only some people were chosen by God to receive the grace of salvation and the rest of humanity was to be judged for its essentially sinful nature. Dear me, no, that's too harsh. There's that judgement I didn't like. Pelagius felt we were *all* fundamentally good, and that if we fell off the wagon, as it were, if we "sinned", redemption was about returning to our (good) senses.

While reading Newell, I bought *The Philosophy of John Scottus Eriugena* (Dermot Moran), wanting to know more about this philosopher's thinking. He arrived several centuries after Pelagius, an Irish theologian circa 800-877 CE. Eriugena referred to sin as the "soul's forgetfulness". I really liked that way of describing it. Non-judgemental. Sometimes we drift too far away from our core, good selves, but it's something we can never lose. In this way, being inauthentic is a sin, as is "being forgetful of who you are, living out of ignorance instead of wisdom, fear instead of love, and fantasy instead of reality". Add to the list, "not making use of the spiritual resources implanted at the heart of your being". So when we are false or selfish, the Celtic tradition sees this failure as not human nature, but a distortion of it. This made sense to me.

By the first week of January 2009 we had finished exploring the seven chapters of *The Book of Creation* and discussed Eriugena through letters and a couple of "coffee and cats" meetings. We had exchanged views on questions like what is truth? (big topic for Eriugena), and discussed the co-existence of the spiritual and material worlds. I was forming the view that the spiritual world is something you ultimately *feel*, rather than know. We agreed that all the arts were key to expressing the full richness of experience. However, Colin felt it was poetry in particular that helps us hold together and to integrate perceiving and conceiving.

In one letter to Colin where I'm reflecting on the fundamental goodness of all nature, I write:

I have been thinking about truth and have concluded that truth is not "out there", "in church" or "in a book", it is actually "in here", inside each of us...

If Augustine was alive today I would send him a quote from Kahlil Gibran, who, when writing on self-knowledge in The Prophet, *says:*

Say not 'I have found the truth', but rather 'I have found a truth'.

Say not 'I have found the path of the soul', say rather 'I have met the soul walking upon my path'.

For the soul walks upon all paths.

The soul walks not upon a line, neither does it grow like a reed.

The soul unfolds itself, like a lotus of countless petals.

Going into spring I found myself growing more and more comfortable with all the fabulous spiritual literature that was available. This surprised me. I had never thought myself intellectual enough to read philosophy, let alone discuss it. In fact, I had always felt intimidated by this subject. But by the summer I found myself writing things like:

*...usually we look at and analyse our world based upon what we know, for example, planet Earth in relation to the sun and other planets (and Eriugena was interested in the cosmos). Or by people relative to territory/the movement of people/power. Or by technology and scientific (i.e. proven) knowledge or economics. Thus we derive systems from knowledge. Eriugena, however, takes a step further and attempts to incorporate what we **do not** know into a system or state of being, rather than leave it out on the basis we do not know. It is back to this complex concept that knowing and not knowing is one and the same (I am still grappling with this!).*

I cannot explain how helpful it was, during my grieving process, to have this outlet for making sense of the world and myself in it. Francesca was there in every step, every letter, every "coffee and cats" along the way. We eventually left Eriugena and went back in time again to the philosophy of Plotinus (205-270 CE, born in Roman Egypt but taught in Rome most of his life), who offered another way of thinking about the relationship between the material world and what he called "the One", "the Source", and how we humans connect to it. I found his thoughts on what happens when we die particularly comforting:

...at body's demise life departs, ready to form and inform other bodies or, ultimately, to retire to union with the universe, and *nothing of real being is ever cancelled.*

So, if we come from Source and return to Source, then Francesca is everywhere – she is in me and around me. There is, in fact, no line drawn, no border to cross. It all simply *is*. That is not to say I didn't miss her terribly, because I did, and still do, every day.

Over the next three years our spiritual exploration stayed with Eriugena and Plotinus, eventually joined by John Habgood (*The Concept of Nature*) and Martin Heidegger, although the frequency of the letters and meetings decreased as life evolved. By March 2013 our spiritual dialogue had come to a natural end and I sent Colin a final thank you letter. I thanked him for his patience, kindness and knowledge. I thanked him for his time, the coffee, and of course, the cats. He will never know how much he helped me start to heal because there are no words to express it. The word gratitude doesn't seem enough. He was my first spiritual teacher and sent me on my way alert to new ideas.

We remain friends, and since he retired from the Church, we meet up once in a while for a general "life check-in". Ione and Petra have both returned to Source.

It is better to strive in one's own dharma than to
succeed in the dharma of another.
Nothing is ever lost in following one's own
dharma...
Bhagavad Gita 3.35

Chapter 3: From corporate to counselling

"Don't let the door hit you in the ass as you walk out". Isn't that the saying when you can't leave somewhere fast enough? It didn't for me. When I left that London office building for the last time I was sure of foot and had pace. I didn't look back once, stepping lightly down the steps onto the street and taking the familiar route along my well-trodden path to Green Park tube station. It was the closing of twelve years of being a corporate animal, and just over a year since Francesca died. I was five months into the spiritual dialogue with Colin.

In the end, it wasn't leaving the company that had been hard, but rather losing my financial independence. My corporate story began when Francesca was 1 ½ years old and Karina had just turned five. Malcolm had lost his job around the time of Francesca's birth and couldn't find other work. We were strapped financially, relying on benefits. It just wasn't a sustainable existence. Although we lurched from one health crisis to the next, Francesca seemed to cling to life and we needed to move on from waiting-for-her-to-die. Given the big age gap, it was more likely that I could get a job faster, but it meant a complete role reversal. As previously explained, it was with huge reluctance that I embarked on that course, especially since we had agreed right from the outset that I would be the one looking after any children we had and he work full time. And leaving a man at home in his mid-fifties with two small children, one with serious disabilities? It was incredibly hard. He didn't relish the prospect either. But needs must, we were desperate, so I went to the local job agency and signed up. I had a degree but no specific training, so any general office work would have to do.

The only thing immediately available was a short period of holiday cover for someone working in the Human Resources department of a large company whose head office was located a short drive away. I took it without hesitation. The lady who met me on the agreed day and who was going on the holiday turned out to be my saviour. She was lovely and so kind as I explained my situation. She explained what I needed to do while she was away and I was determined to do my best in her absence. Two weeks later she returned and was happy with how things had gone. I asked her to please bear me in mind if anything else came up. I did some more cover and finally had a lucky break. The department was looking for some full-time help which I applied for and successfully got. It was a two-year contract position in HR as an assistant, which meant that I could not join the pension scheme or share scheme, nor get private health cover. That could only happen if I became a permanent employee. But beggars can't be choosers and I was just so relieved and grateful to be offered the opportunity. Finally, some financial stability.

The worst part was being away from the girls every day, though. I missed them. Francesca was too young to really take on board the shift, but not so her older sister. Karina and I were very close, and I knew she found the separation difficult. It was a huge adjustment for us all but we made it work.

During the next eighteen months I moved around HR doing various roles but realised this part of the business didn't suit me. I had a sense of urgency of finding a career path with prospects, because the current pay was low and not really enough to support a family of four. I needed to move up. I tried applying for other jobs in the building but it soon became clear that moving between departments was unlikely, you basically had to stay in your box. However, I did get, and enjoy, a job as assistant in Public Affairs, a wing of HR. This was a small team that dealt with the public relations, the company's external face. This was more varied and interesting, and I especially enjoyed being responsible for the charitable donation budget. This involved assessing and choosing local projects to sponsor, for example, in primary and secondary schools, charities and cultural events. It got me out and about in the community.

The money continued to be a problem, though. Then came my second lucky break. This local head office was part of a bigger corporation based in London that decided to host an external meeting presenting our business to financial analysts from the City. The person who was responsible for running the show spent a few days with our department preparing the event. I enjoyed helping her out. When the event was over the daily work routine resumed. A few weeks later my manager called me into her office and said there was an opening as an assistant in the London office, working for this person who had run the event. I had been noticed. It would mean an increase in salary, but more importantly there was the prospect of upward movement.

The only problem was that I would have to commute to and from London every day, leaving the house at 6.45 am and not getting back until 6.45 pm. Twelve hours away. I would miss even more time with the girls and the day would be even longer and tougher for Malcolm. It was another tough choice. In the end the finances decided, we needed more money.

At first the adjustment in routine was awful, both mother and father became that much more tired. However, I worked hard and applied myself, getting a couple of promotions that gave me a meaningful salary. Two years later we were able to move out of our little two-bedroom flat on top of a converted old Edwardian house next to a busy main road to a lovely four-bedroom rental in the middle of the countryside just to the south. It was an ideal place for the girls, and I knew the local schooling was good from the visits I had made when wearing my corporate sponsor hat.

The department I was now working in was the public face to the company's investors, shareholders and financial analysts, called Investor Relations. It meant I had had to get myself up to speed with the financial world and speak the language of balance sheets, PE ratios and analyst spreadsheets. It also meant I needed to know everything about the company's products – the science, the product marketplace and the competition. Now, I'm the type of person that if I'm going to do something I'm going to do it well, I give it 100%. I made it my priority to learn and remember pretty much all aspects of the company. I had the whole Research and Development pipeline in my head. This made sense to me since I was asked questions about, and was expected to know the answers to, all aspects of the business. Within the team I was dubbed the "encyclopaedic memory".

The years passed and looking in from the outside you would probably call me successful. But was it really *me*? This corporate being? Sometimes I was plagued by self-doubt, terrified of being asked a question and not knowing the answer. In business meetings I was often the only woman in the room. The financial world is an intimidating and unforgiving place, regularly chewing up and spitting out people who couldn't handle the pressure. I couldn't be one of them. This environment of handling share price sensitive information all the time was stressful to the say the least.

There were some great moments, though. Given the nature of our communications, our department worked closely with the senior executives, which was a huge privilege. Being present in key internal meetings where important decisions were made was interesting and exciting. When preparing for an external analyst presentation one time, I was supporting the current head of R & D who would be speaking at the event. He had noticed my head for detail and good memory. There I was, in a hall somewhere in the City of London, all the senior executives gathered with over a hundred financial analysts and investors, and he was asked a question in the Q&A session. Out of nowhere he just smiled and said, "Mina probably knows the answer to that question." I nearly fell off my chair! He then went on and answered, of course, but I just really appreciated the compliment. And for the record, I did know the answer to that question.

But nothing stays the same. There had been some management changes which meant that by the time Francesca died, I no longer had the work and responsibilities that I had enjoyed. So when it came to the crunch, the decision to leave was easy. Placing my resignation letter on my manager's desk and watching him read it felt satisfying and right. I did have a good ending, however. I was hugely honoured to have the CEO turn up to my leaving-do and acknowledge my work contribution.

It was also clear to me that I didn't want to pursue the same job type in a different company. My corporate job had been a means to an end, to support my family and be the sole breadwinner. It was not my calling, though. I was in a different personal situation now, in a new relationship in which the financial pressure was off. My bereavement had profoundly shaken my roots and made me question what my purpose was. With Hamish offering to take over the finances fully, I was fortunate to have the opportunity to choose. I needed to go in another direction and leave the capital city in the rear-view mirror.

It was not in my nature to be rash or lackadaisical. I always needed a plan. The prospect of losing my income, which I had fought so hard to establish, was incentive enough to actively find a new career. Looking at a blank piece of paper on which to flesh out other options was quite scary, I mean, what else could I actually do? While I was still working in London, I had been researching other professions and felt drawn towards counselling. I knew I had an affinity for understanding people and their issues. I also believed that my life experience at that point, of loss and overcoming hardship, could be of use in helping others. Perhaps this was something I could build on?

I discovered that there were different counselling theories and read up on them all. For example, Person-centred, Cognitive Behavioural Therapy and Gestalt to name a few. It was important to find the right fit. But I was drawn towards the

Psychodynamic method originated by Sigmund Freud and later expanded by Carl Jung and Erik Erikson. The idea that we are driven by unconscious forces originating in childhood experiences resonated with me. However, to be certain it was the right thing, I applied to do a part-time one-year general certificate in counselling with a counselling organisation in London. The class was held in the evenings so I could go there directly after work.

Suddenly I was thrown into a group of completely different people from all walks of life. Different cultures, different professions, young and old. My existence to date had been very narrow and consisted of three points: corporate office (with some business travel), home in southern county small town and paediatric hospital wards. I rarely veered off this triangular track. It was an eye opener to interact with the broader world.

The course covered basic counselling skills like listening, reflecting, building rapport and the use of questions, but also included what was called an experiential group. The broader group was split into these smaller groups which met outside of the main class. Each group had a facilitator, a professional counsellor. Well, nothing could have prepared me for this. We would gather in a room and wait for someone to say something. The facilitator didn't lead the meeting in any way, there was no agenda. We started as complete strangers but then over time the stories would emerge and we would get a sense of each other, where we came from and what was going on for us. Gradually it

51

became clear that we pressed each other's buttons as deeper feelings emerged. We were encouraged to keep it honest and authentic.

It was here that for the first time I had my "corporate animal" persona reflected back at me and it wasn't nice. Turning up in a business suit with my business travel suitcase apparently had an air of arrogance and privilege, I was told. I was intimidating, overbearing and overconfident, apparently. Wow, it was quite the shock. It was certainly not who I was *inside*, the mum at home playing with and hugging my girls. These qualities they perceived and disliked worked well in the business world. Perhaps, unconsciously, I had developed this aspect to survive. Had my exterior protective shell become too hard? Upsetting though it was, I realised this was the outcome of how much I had compartmentalised my life. I had never let my domestic issues spill into the workplace. Just a handful of people had known about Francesca and what I was dealing with at home, because sometimes I'd have to leave the office suddenly to join Francesca in a hospital emergency. In fact, many colleagues were shocked to hear of her death because they had not known about my personal life. The hard shell had been effective.

The experiential group experience sounds brutal, perhaps, but it was critical. It kick-started the personal growth process of self-discovery. Of finding my way back to *me*. I allowed myself to open up a little and eventually shared with the group the loss of Francesca, because it was hard to be authentic and honest withholding it. Also, I felt the facilitator had a good, solid containing presence. She had a Black-African background and radiated an unspoken *knowing*. Her energy emanated wisdom and something more, it was hard to describe. I hadn't encountered it before. Like a connection to something deeper, beyond this dimension, but I couldn't put my finger on it.

One experiential evening I felt particularly emotional about Francesca and broke down. My spiritual crisis was at a peak.

"Why did she have to die? Why? How could it have happened?" I wept.

The facilitator was completely calm and serene and simply said, "She was only meant to be here a short time."

"But I don't understand!" I replied, sobbing.

She said nothing more, remaining perfectly quiet and still. It wasn't something she could explain. I took the hint that I would have to figure it out for myself.

By the time I decided to resign, I knew I wanted to pursue counselling as a career and follow the psychodynamic path. Since I would no longer be in London, I could look for training where I lived. When I received my Certificate in Counselling Skills the following summer in 2009, I applied for a two-year diploma course run by a local counselling service and was delighted when I got accepted.

This diploma course also included an experiential group element. As you can imagine, I was glad to have been initiated into this way of working, but none of the others knew what it was.

They had all done the one-year certificate together and I was the only new person to join the class. Because they had already formed bonds, friendships and alliances, the experiential meetings were mostly filled with polite conversation and chit-chat. I noticed that this facilitator was more like an observer and didn't encourage deeper exploration of what came up in the moment for people. This really wasn't edgy London at all, I was in the provinces now. But eventually I did come up against myself with a lady called Joanna.

I don't remember exactly when it started but early on I became aware that the dynamic between us was difficult. There was something about her that I found very painful. When she spoke it felt jarring, sometimes to the point where I wanted to leave the room. And she was wary of me. What was going on?

The great thing about the experiential setting is that there is no escape in the sense that you have to keep coming back to the meetings. Sure, you can choose to not face the issues, you're not forced to talk, but you have to attend, to be there and sit with whatever is going on. I decided to be brave and face the stuff that kept coming up for me with Joanna but the training group was not the right place. I instinctively knew we had to work this out between us. So, I contacted her outside of class and suggested we meet for a chat. Luckily, she agreed and we did. It turned out to be one of those pivotal turning points, when you take the risk, roll the dice and receive the reward.

We met regularly and over time revealed each other's full stories. It turned out that our life experiences were remarkably, even spookily, similar. Dysfunctional family background, unavailable parents, sibling rivalry, child bereavement, divorce. We had both been put through the mill one way or another but had found the strength to survive. You would think that we would naturally get on like a house on fire! What was the issue then? I discovered the problem was how I perceived Joanna. Over the years, I had become defended and hard to protect myself, presenting to the world an I-am-coping, I-am-managing, I-am-strong façade. Joanna on the other hand was emotionally more open, softer. I interpreted this as vulnerability and weakness, and if there was something I couldn't bear, it was exactly that. Weakness. There had been no room for weakness in my story as far back as I could remember, well before Francesca's arrival. I always had to cope and get on, no one had been that interested in what I thought or felt. When I felt I encountered it in others it triggered resentment and intolerance but I hadn't consciously made the connection.

At the same time, my strong "coping vibe" pressed a button for Joanna who was sensitive to being judged as someone who couldn't manage, a feeling rooted in her history. We concluded that we were bouncing off each other's stuff. In other words, our issue wasn't actually about each other at all, it was about *ourselves*. And this was Joanna's biggest gift to me – the eye-opening discovery that when we think we encounter something challenging in someone else that triggers pain, we are in fact encountering a part of ourselves we don't like or don't want to accept. We're looking in the mirror.

Colin had awakened me on an intellectual level, but it was through Joanna I began to open up my *heart*, to soften both to myself and to others. To accept my own vulnerability. Because being brave all the time was extremely exhausting, I can tell you. Over the years we became each other's rock as life presented us with new challenges and tests. And Joanna offered me other precious gifts: trust and female love.

To trust is to be vulnerable. It can spill over into dependency, something else I "don't do". And the risk is disappointment and pain, if and when someone lets you down. If this happens repeatedly, in the end you're not going to take the risk in the first place to protect yourself from that pain. With Joanna I felt I could take the risk. I could show her every dark corner of my flip side and it was okay. I could expose my wounds and it was okay. I told her how it felt to hear Francesca's last breath and hold her lifeless, heavy body in my arms and she bore it. I could cry and shout about how unfair life was and she heard it (what a dog walk that was! Fortunately, we were in a wood on our own where no one else could hear). She gave me permission to *collapse*. Equally, when family issues past and present reared up for Joanna, I strengthened her resolve to face them rather than fall into old detrimental patterns. We could be "messy" for each other.

And out of this trust I was able to experience a deep love for another woman for the first time. This is not the sexual kind at all, don't get me wrong. No, this is the love that comes from feeling really and truly *known* by someone else. Being fully *seen*. The fact it was a female is significant because my relationship with my mother was such that I had a natural distrust of women (long story). It is hard to explain how huge, how significant, this shift was for me but let's just say it was life-changing. It offered more healing for my shattered heart.

I enjoyed working with adult clients at the counselling service but at some point I became interested in working with young people. Being a parent to an adolescent at this time meant I was tuned into that age group, I had an understanding of the issues. And I enjoyed their company and youthful energy. I kept an eye open for such a job opportunity and luckily spotted one not long after. It was a volunteer placement at a charity that offered free counselling to children and young people age 11 – 25, including working at local schools. It meant a 50-minute drive there and back, but that was doable. I applied and was thrilled to get the job.

Working with young people proved very different to counselling adults. Less reflecting and analysing the past and more dealing with issues happening at the moment. The source of their problems was in the *now*. It was raw, tough, often heart breaking and shocking but at the same time they showed such resilience, courage and willingness to change. They had no idea how inspiring they were. You could make a lot of progress in a surprisingly short time once trust was established. The work was varied as one could imagine – self harm, bullying, bereavement, young carers, abuse, drugs. But I was privileged to work with a few autistic clients who opened up a view of the world I had not been aware of before: *the spectrum*.

The 18-year-old young man was diagnosed with some kind of "social anxiety disorder". I say "some kind" because when I looked into it, there turned out to be a plethora of autistic categories and countless labels. Fortunately, being a counsellor and not a psychiatrist, I was able to avoid being drawn into, and probably getting lost in, the definitions and simply work with "what there is". Work with the person in the room. The approach was the same for all the other clients – listening, accepting without judgement and trying to see the world through their eyes.

He was highly anxious and preferred to sit in long silences sometimes, just gathering his thoughts. He had two main concerns that were causing him distress – how he could get a job and how to tell when someone was upset. We spent time identifying and discussing his feelings and how they were triggered. We worked through some coping strategies. At one point I thought it would help him manage his anxiety if we role played a job interview scenario so he could feel more confident when interviewed for a job in a hotel he had applied for.

Me: So, let's pretend you're at the hotel now and I'm the hotel manager who is going to ask you some questions. We can stop any time to see how you're feeling.

Big pause, eyes staring at me.

Him: But I know you….

We started to laugh! It was so funny and we could both see it. Of course, what was I thinking? He took everything literally, that was part of the problem. To imagine, to pretend, to act was alien to him, it was a game he couldn't play in any shape or form. I really understood him then, understood how hard it was for him to make sense of a world in which people hinted, assumed, played mind games, manipulated, joked, were sarcastic, said things they didn't mean, were vague or unclear, made promises they didn't keep, had personal agendas and so on. No wonder he felt anxious, isolated and *different*. I tried to help him accept this difference, *his* difference. He found that hard because at the end of the day he just wanted to fix himself and be able to function normally. Accepting that he would never be like everyone else was understandably hard.

Another client was 16 years old and presented with "depression". When she first walked into the room I was struck by her beauty – shiny auburn hair framing an open face with large blue eyes and milky skin. The overriding feeling emanating from her was sadness. She had been referred to the Child and Adolescent Mental Health Services (CAMHS) due to behavioural issues and promptly put on anti-depressants. It seemed her family had labelled her as "a bit of a drama queen" and hard to get along with, and she also had issues at school. I managed to piece it together as she described her life. She found some classrooms at school intolerable to be in, for example, the science lab with the high ceiling and high stools to sit on. The sound and light in there made it impossible for her to concentrate. She worked in a pub at the weekend and said how she loved serving in the part of the building with low ceilings and enclosed spaces but felt uncomfortable in the modern bit which was more open.

Her: Do you know where my favourite place to be is?

Me: No, where is that?

Her: A railway carriage with compartments. I feel safe inside the compartment.

One time she arrived for her session looking particularly bright and I acknowledged it verbally.

Her: Yes, today is a good day because it's Tuesday and Tuesdays are green.

Me: Really, that's interesting. Do the days of the week have different colours?

Her: Yes they do.

And she proceeded to explain the colours of the days, relating each colour to a mood. It was fascinating. When I looked up this relationship with colours I discovered *synesthesia*, which is a condition associated with autism where people experience a mixing of senses such as "hearing" tastes and shapes, or "seeing" numbers or words in colours. It turned out she was very sensitive to colour, for example, she found it hard to read and write on white paper, it was too jarring for her brain.

We discussed how she could manage that better, like using a different colour note paper and pens for her schoolwork and colour coding her files in a way that made sense to her. I also tried to empower her by encouraging her to explain to the school these feelings so she could get support, rather than let herself be labelled as "difficult". I felt angry that this lovely young woman had been so misunderstood and put on medication. She was autistic, not mentally ill. We didn't have long to work together and I sincerely hope I managed to shift her view of herself.

Me: You know, there is nothing wrong with you. You are not sick. You are just different, you see and interpret things differently.

Her: I know.

Me: I don't think you need the medication. You could consider discussing this with your doctor, you are old enough to do that.

Her: It's just easier for the adults if I take the pills.

I had to leave it there, and I could see why she wasn't ready to take on the adults at home and at the educational institutions. I hoped, however, that we managed to make some progress with her self-acceptance and self-confidence, similar to the client work with the young autistic man. But this whole thing of drugging our youth to make life easier for the grown-ups...dear oh dear.

After four years of volunteer and paid work at the youth charity, the long round-trip commute became too tiring and I yearned for a job closer to home. Once again, I was lucky and soon an opening came up as Lead Counsellor at the local secondary school. I crossed everything, fingers and toes, to get it – it would mean a 5-minute drive down the road. The universe was kind and the job was offered to me. It was a significant step up, I would be responsible for two other counsellors and the smooth running of a school counselling service that had been established for eight years and open every day of the week. We worked at full capacity with a long waiting list that never shortened.

As expected, the issues were similar to those I had encountered at the other schools. Navigating through adolescence is a challenging process at the best of times and for some just too painful without support.

One morning I was at my desk in the open plan room with another colleague present. The door suddenly swung open and a schoolboy marched in and stopped just inside the room.

"This morning is not going at all well for me!" With that, he turned on his heel and walked out again.

I glanced over at my colleague.

"Classic Asperger's," she said knowingly with a smile and carried on with her work.

Asperger's? I hadn't encountered that in my work to date and wasn't specifically familiar with it. I remembered the autistic clients in the past, though, and knew it was on the autistic spectrum. There was something about how that boy entered and exited the room, what he said and the way he said it, that caused a flicker of something at the back of my mind. But I couldn't grasp it and in a moment it was gone.

Sadly, the job was not to last. Having started in September of that academic year, the following May 2015 I was told by the counselling agency (through whom the school paid for the service) that the headmaster had decided to shut the whole service down. Just like that, no discussion, no slimming it down to two days, or even just one day a week. Apparently the school budget had been massively hit by a drop in educational funding by the government and something had to be cut. It has always been, and will always be, a mystery to me how support for school students' emotional and mental wellbeing is classified as some sort of extra "nice to have" and not *essential*. How are children supposed to get the most from their schooling if they are mentally and emotionally disadvantaged? They won't get the results that truly reflect their ability, which in turn will affect their future job prospects. This is criminal to me, frankly. And all that happens is that the mental health problem for the young person worsens, the cost escalates, and has to be borne by the health service. Which cannot cope because it is oversubscribed and underfunded. On and on it goes. Nobody wins, the person and society lose. But a small intervention at relatively little cost when the issue arises at school age could make all the difference.

Anyway, it was what it was. I spent a very stressful summer term ending with clients, supporting the other counsellors ending with their clients, and cleaning out all the historic and current paperwork. By the end of it I was on my knees – exhausted, angry, sad, but most of all disillusioned. Disillusioned with my school counsellor profession. The institutions that needed to value it and pay for it simply didn't. End of story. It wasn't just the local school either, it turned out that the other secondary schools I had worked at in my previous job had also withdrawn their counselling funding.

At the same time I also felt relieved if I'm honest. I was dealing with high stress levels before the announcement came about closing the service and had wondered how long I could manage. Now, the decision had been taken out of my hands.

For the first time in my life I decided to stop. To pause. To not immediately chase some new plan. I was tired and had no energy or inclination to rush into something else. Maybe that was why it had happened and I was meant to leave that professional track. Instead, I allowed myself a year to just be and see what developed.

Would something come to me of its own accord if I let it, if I created the space? If I was not a corporate animal or a counsellor, what was I then?

*"Through selfless service, you will always be
fruitful and find the fulfilment of your desires":
this is the promise of the Creator.
Bhagavad Gita 3.10*

Chapter 4: An appointment made by God

That last spring of working as a school counsellor had been made bearable by our regular visit to Uganda in February. Hamish and I spent a week in the now familiar Jinja, the second largest city in Uganda built on the shore of Lake Victoria. It was our third trip to this beautiful country and on the long-haul flight heading due south, my thoughts returned to our first arrival there four years before.

"Oh my god, are all those *mosquitoes*?"
Karina's eyes were as big as saucers.
It was 22.30 local time and the lamps hanging on the outside of the airport terminal building cast pools of light into the vast African darkness. In the battle between light and dark, dark was definitely winning, the lamps seemed to struggle with the effort of cutting into the thick night. But in this light, you could see the silhouette of millions, perhaps billions, of insects, some scarily large. A

dense flying mass jostling to get close to the bright lightbulbs. As we gingerly walked down the steps that had been wheeled to the side of the plane, I followed her gaze and found my eyes opening as wide as hers.

"Most likely," I replied, keeping my voice steady. The runway at Entebbe was literally on the edge of Lake Victoria, plenty of water for all manner of bitey things to thrive.

I knew what her concern was, that edge in her voice. Malaria. We had talked a lot about this as we planned the trip. Hamish, Karina and I were fairly well travelled, but when we looked at the list of vaccinations we needed to have and the anti-malarial tablets we had to start taking a couple of days before departure, we knew already this was going to be a different sort of travel experience. A bit *hanging out there*.

Yet nothing prepared me for my first arrival in this part of the world. The aeroplane door opened and I stepped out into an infinite night sky that felt like it could swallow me up. The cosmos was so close, bearing down upon me, it was tempting to reach up and try to touch some of the millions of twinkling, winking stars. The overriding feeling was one of awe. My awareness was then drawn to the warmth of the air caressing my skin. Seconds later I sensed a deep, earthy, slightly intoxicating smell entering my nose. It was an intense all-at-once multisensory experience. My whole body, my entire Being, was suddenly fully awake and alert in spite of the long nine-hour plane ride.

"Good thing we're taking the meds," I added to be reassuring. But we both reached into our hand luggage for mosquito repellent at the same time, applying it liberally to any exposed skin.

The only thing I knew about Entebbe was the famous raid that took place here in 1976 when Israeli commandos freed hostages taken by terrorists. Hardly a comforting thought. So why were the three of us standing in the immigration queue here? The connection was through the company I had worked for in London. In that job I had got to know the senior executives, and the wife of one of them was involved with an educational charity supporting schools and orphanages in Jinja. It sounded like a good cause and I was keen to help, so I set up a monthly donation. Hamish and I also attended their fund-raising events where we learned more about the activities of the Jinja Educational Trust (JET). I got to know this lady personally, as we kept in touch after I left the company.

In one of our many conversations talking about JET's various projects she said, "Why don't you go out there and see for yourself how your money is being spent? You know, follow your money? You would love it."

Indeed, why not? My sense of adventure was piqued. The timing fitted nicely with Karina's gap year, so she could come with us. I put the suggestion to them. Yes, they were both up for it!

Back at Entebbe airport, we collected our bags, laden with supplies for the charity, and exited baggage claim hoping that the driver booked for us would be there. It was one of those travel "what if he doesn't show up" moments which I tried not to dwell on. The good news was, he was indeed standing there waiting, with a big smile, holding aloft a sign with our name on it. The bad news was that we seemed to have walked into a military siege. Was there another hostage crisis we didn't know about? Armed soldiers were everywhere, cradling machine guns. And as we joined the road leading out of the airport we saw long lines of army trucks parked along the roadside as far as the eye could see. It felt somewhere between intimidating and terrifying. I had known beforehand we were coming out of our comfort zone, but this?

"What on earth is going on?" I asked the driver. We had a 3 ½ hour drive ahead of us to Jinja where we would arrive in the middle of the night.

"Oh, it's the presidential elections in a couple of days. It's always like this then." He was clearly unconcerned and quite relaxed.

Really? This was *normal*? Well, this was a presentation of democracy I was not familiar with. It had the air of an impending coup, if you asked me. But this was Africa, not the cosy First World.

I had to laugh at myself though. No wonder the plane had been so empty, we had been so pleased to spread out and have space. In our naivety we hadn't "read the memo", hadn't done due diligence, and booked the trip as if we were going to Berlin or something. Instead, we arrived in Uganda at the most risky time possible. I just shook my head with a wry smile at the thought. It was too late now. I think this was the first moment I felt the impulse to properly and fully let go. Let go of everything. Us. The trip. I mean, we were clearly not in control. I simply had to accept that the next couple of weeks were in the lap of the gods. We were travelling "hopefully". And yet it was actually kind of liberating to be honest. For the first time since Francesca died I could allow myself to go with the flow. What was the point in sitting here in this four-wheel-drive van roaring through Entebbe towards Kampala and worrying? I knew we would be okay. Francesca would surely look out for us.

So instead I turned my attention to the fascinating views passing by the car window. I quickly became absorbed by the late-night street life on the road to the capital, where we would turn right and head due east to our destination. It was a sight to behold. In spite of the army presence, thick throngs of people mingled inside and outside wooden and corrugated iron shacks that sat right on the edge of the road. Loud clubbing music emanated from some of them, I could just catch glimpses of flashing multicoloured disco lights. There were motorcycles everywhere, darting through the busy traffic or gathered in big groups on street corners, the drivers chatting with each other. These were taxi scooters of some kind, I could see people hopping on and off the back of them for payment.

This lively scene seemed to go on forever but the city eventually receded behind us, the road side quietened as we passed through smaller communities. Then suddenly we were plunged into darkness with no one in sight. We were driving through the thick jungle forest that lies between Kampala and Jinja. All was quiet and still except for the noise of the van engine. I could only just see the faint outline of the huge trees on either side of the road against the night sky.

All at once we came to a halt and found ourselves staring into the torch light of some armed soldiers manning a security checkpoint. My heart started to pound uncontrollably in my chest. I mean, out here anything could happen and no one would ever know… But we were soon on our way. The driver remained relaxed as ever. Finally the road came out at the River Nile where we crossed over the top of the dam and into Jinja. We noted a huge water cannon, presumably ready for crowd control, sitting in the middle of a roundabout with some sleepy soldiers nearby, but were too tired to react. It was 3.00 am and all we wanted to do was lie horizontal as soon as we arrived at the hotel. Getting ready for bed at last, we noticed, but tried to ignore, the holes in the mosquito nets which themselves were too short to be tucked under the beds. More liberal application of insect repellent followed.

We had only rested for a few hours before it was time to get up. Whatever sleep we had got was fitful, we were still pretty wired from the journey and the foreignness of the environment. We had heard the packs of wild domestic dogs roaming the streets in the night, which was a bit unnerving. I concluded that there would be a lot to get used to on this trip, but that was part of the deal.

At breakfast we mused on the fact that the fruit and coffee at the buffet had been grown just miles from where we sat. The intensity of flavour was palpable on the tongue, I had never tasted such sweet bananas and pineapple before. As we ate, I could sense the warmth of the night giving way to searing heat. I realised that the thing about being right on the Equator (Jinja is only a few feet in the northern hemisphere) was that the sun was always fully "on", right on top of you. Unforgiving. Equally, the shadows were very dark and harsh. But we had a programme to follow, so it was on with the hats and the sunscreen. We were collected by Godfrey, the local manager of the charity and our host for the visit.

As we drove towards the town centre we were finally able to really *see* Africa. Like the arrival at Entebbe, it was an instant sensory overload and culture shock. It's hard to describe what strikes you first. The light that is so bright it feels like your eyeballs are being sliced by shards of glass? That intoxicating smell of the red earth awakening some deep-seated primal instinct? The dilapidated and often abandoned government-style buildings that had seen better days in colonial times? The blatant lack of infrastructure as displayed by the appalling state of the potholed streets and litter strewn everywhere?

The myriad of impressions meeting my gaze through the car window made me reflect on this country's history. Similar to most of modern Africa, it's a rough story. Unlike Kenya, Uganda had been a British Protectorate from 1894 to 1962, not a colony. This meant the people here had been able to exercise a higher degree of self-governance, and the transition to independent nation had been relatively smooth. Aside from the smattering of colonial architecture (think cream stucco, lots of pillars and columns, one-storey high), the only other nod to British influence was English as the official language (Swahili was added in 2005) and the presence of British electrical plug sockets in the walls. Handy for us of course.

Unfortunately, Uganda fell the same way as many of its neighbours, into military dictatorship in the form of General Idi Amin. He deposed Milton Obote, the Prime Minister chosen by the British, in 1971. What followed was eight years of internal carnage, including the ousting of 60,000 Asians and the destruction of the economy. The horror of this period was brought to life by Godfrey's stories of the time. He had been a small child when Uganda was created and a teenager when the Idi Amin coup happened. He said that at one point there were so many dead bodies floating down the River Nile that the dam at Jinja got gummed up. Impossible to imagine. Responding to our observations of pot holes so large a whole car could fall in, Godfrey said the country was still recovering from this terrible history and subsequent economic mismanagement. The proof was in the statistics: average life expectancy for a male 60 years, female 65 years, infant mortality rate at 34% and consistent leader of the highest maternal mortality rate in the world – one in every 49 women dying due to complications in pregnancy or childbirth. AIDS, malaria and the lack of access to clean water lay behind the numbers.

It was hard to not feel overwhelmed. And yet, as we got out of the car at the top of the main street and started walking towards the central thoroughfare, you were struck by *life*. Yes, life everywhere, busy shops, street sellers and traffic (mostly the numerous and loud *Boda-Boda* motorcycle taxis). But most of all it was the beauty of the people that got my attention. The women in particular were stunning, it was hard not to stare. No make-up required for them. This impression was further enhanced by bright colours everywhere, in the clothes, the street art and the gifts for sale. However, we were struck by the absence of any old people. I couldn't spot any grey or white hair anywhere, the statistics sadly seemed to be true.

It was approaching noon on this first day, and the heat along with the lingering sleep deprivation made for hard going as we marched down the seemingly endless street. Godfrey was keen to show and tell us everything.

Suddenly he came to a halt, pausing in front of a man of short stature who had been walking towards us. The two men clearly knew each other, greeting each other warmly. It was a display of the traditional Ugandan greeting that we would come to know. You take the other's hand in both of yours, and they do the same. You stand there, hands clasped and squeezing with constant pressure, looking straight and directly into each other's eyes as you speak, either introducing yourself or engaging in immediate conversation. You remain interlocked like this for some time, long enough for it to become uncomfortable if you are a non-tactile

Westerner. Personally, I loved it. These people took the time to really *see* the person, properly connect, give each other their full attention. It was totally authentic. In any case, the three of us had to greet Godfrey's friend in turn, in the African way, as Godfrey introduced him to us and vice versa.

"This is my dear friend Father Leonard. Father Leonard, these are my guests from England."

He may have been short, we towered over him, but Father Leonard had a huge presence. The sun gleamed on his bald head, glistening in the tiny beads of perspiration, but he seemed unbothered by the 30°C+ temperature dressed as he was in a thick three-piece brown suit with collared shirt and tie. His wide smile beamed from ear to ear. I was trying not to faint, the heat felt like it was pushing me into the ground.

"Ah, England! How very nice, very nice indeed for you to come here and visit us! I'm so very pleased to meet you," he said enthusiastically.

We thanked him, totally taken in by his charm. It was impossible to not smile back. Individual greetings done, he raised his right hand and pointed up to the sky.

"This," pausing, looking at all of us, "has been an appointment made by God!"

The heat had got to him after all, I thought. But he continued with his little sermon unperturbed.

"You see, when you meet someone you know without having arranged it, that's God's doing, it's a gift from Him. So you must always stop to check what the meeting offers you. And by stopping to greet my friend Godfrey here, I have now met all of you special people who have come all the way from England!"

I loved this guy, what an important message for us all. He was quite right of course. I felt a tinge of shame at all the times I had not done this, bumping into people and quickly making my excuses in order to rush off. One assumes there will be another opportunity. But here in Uganda they don't necessarily have the luxury of such an assumption, given the constant presence of disease and other threats to life. You take nothing for granted, grateful for every day you had food, shelter and health. No, you jolly well gave that person you met your time.

This theme was to shape the rest of our visit. Wherever we went, whomever we met, we found gratitude, generosity, joy and faith. It was conveyed through the smiles and shy giggles of the school children who stood up in class to greet us and in the firm handshakes of the teaching staff as we toured the schools JET supported to see what it was providing. New classrooms, latrines, water sources, even a cow for one of the primary schools to learn how to look after and provide milk for the children. We in turn had brought with us school supplies – chalk, paper, pencils, educational posters.

It was humbling to chat with the headteachers and their staff and learn how they were making ends meet to give the children the best education they could, in what were fairly challenging circumstances. Some of the classrooms were wooden shacks sitting straight on the earth and open to the elements. No electricity. No clean water.

And yet the children were well disciplined and the teachers respected. There was laughter, lightness and hope hanging in the air. No behavioural policy required here. In Uganda, no matter how poor you are, you have to pay a nominal fee for your child to go to school. We were looking at the lucky ones, although some didn't have the means to wear the school uniform and were essentially dressed in rags. For every child we saw in school, there would be dozens more out there in the streets who would never see the inside of a classroom.

But where my heart was really touched was in the orphanages, of which we visited the three connected to JET. Wow, if you've never felt humbled before, you're going to here, no question. Whatever hard edges you walk in with will be gone when you walk out. You see, something gives, something softens inside as you hold a malnourished baby that was found abandoned in a field, or on the roadside, or on the church steps. Or a baby brought in by a friend of a 13-year-old girl who was raped and is now unable to care for her child physically and/or psychologically. Or the child orphaned by AIDS. You feel the weight of a human life resting in your arms and look into the enormous searching black eyes of this tiny being, which seem to see your very soul. It's a look so delving and deep it makes you wonder who the hell you really are. Are you joyful? Grateful? Generous? Are you really?

But neither the children nor their doting aunties, which is what you called the female staff or stand-in mothers, were victims or tragedies. They didn't want or deserve our pity. These were homes of joy, hope and love. And *life*. Every child here represented one less child abandoned out there, a life saved, a new potential. Life was celebrated daily in the domestic routines, the playtime, the meals, the hugs and kisses. This feeling was reflected in the names given to the children who had arrived nameless and sometimes with no story: Hope, Life, Charity, Grace, Precious, Peace, Mercy, Patience, Gift. Some boys' names reflected the Christian faith of the culture: John, Luke, Matthew, Gabriel, Samuel, Paul.

It was a huge privilege to spend time in these places, offered food (which we always accepted respectfully) and embracing them physically as well as spiritually. The less people had, the more they had to give. The circle of life was real here, not a Disney movie. Birth and death were accepted equally without fear or question. So when I was asked by the orphanage aunties how many children I had, I had permission to be honest, to say I had two but lost one. Instead of recoiling and changing the subject in embarrassment (what I had come to expect at home), the response was a non-verbal look of real empathy accompanied by slow nodding. A *knowing*. I felt such relief at finally being understood and fully *seen*. I didn't need to make my story okay for them. In fact, it felt like it enabled a bonding, a connection between us women.

The days kept coming around and we fell into the African rhythm, having fully acclimatised. As my body and soul unwound and relaxed, I learned to enjoy getting up in the morning with a loose plan and rough timings but not feeling stressed if the schedule went adrift. I noticed that we ended each day having completed what we set out to do but in a different order and times. This was called "Africa time", a bit like we would say "all in good time". There was nothing for it but to let go of the Western inclination to rush, push, or force an agenda. Let go, let go, let go.

The more places and people we visited, the more I saw my own life from a different perspective. All the things we took for granted would be a gift in this part of the world, grabbed with both hands and cherished. What did we really have to complain about? When I reflected on all the privileges I enjoyed - healthcare, further education, access to training, career options, food, clean water – I felt a deeper appreciation for all of it. Because you simply didn't complain about anything as a guest in this country:

No more coffee available at the breakfast buffet? Never mind, you had one cup.

You've waited 1 ½ hrs for your plate of food to arrive? At least you're eating today.

The water coming out of the shower has no pressure and is a funny colour? At least you can clean yourself.

The water isn't safe to drink out of the tap? You've got money to buy bottled.

Can't find any of your favourite foods on the menu? Eat what you get.

You get the idea. Sweat from the heat, sure, but don't sweat the small stuff. Not here.

We had done some tourist things in Jinja during the week, including a boat trip on Lake Victoria to the source of the River Nile. But before returning to the UK we were to go on safari and see more of Uganda along the way. I had booked us four nights at the gorgeous Mweya Lodge in the Queen Elizabeth National Park, an area of natural beauty in the far south-western corner of Uganda, right on the border with the Democratic Republic of the Congo. The local travel agency the charity used allocated us a driver and safari guide who was named Sunday. I wondered whether that denoted a link to an orphanage but didn't ask. In any case, he would take us there and back. Having only seen a town setting so far, I was excited to experience the countryside. We were collected at 5.00 am without any detailed information of the route or real sense of the distance (again, what was I thinking?). However, what a mercy that turned out to be, otherwise we probably wouldn't have embarked on it. To get to the west we had to drive to and through Kampala, but on the other side of the capital the road just ended. Yeah, that's right. The tarmac came to a straight edge across the road and the jeep bumped onto the dirt, and that was it. Idi Amin's legacy. For the next 220 miles we were on a dusty track.

All in, the journey took 12 hours during which our bodies took a bit of a beating. Owing to no electricity in any rural area, and even in most towns, there were no traffic lights anywhere. This meant the only way to slow down traffic was to build massive speed bumps across the road. These were so high and vicious it felt and sounded like the whole undercarriage of the jeep was coming away as we went over them. There was no way of avoiding a big jolt each time. There was no chance of nodding off at any point.

But I didn't want to sleep. In spite of the uncomfortable ride it was an eye-opening experience and I didn't want to miss a thing, I was glued to the window. Africa just kept on coming at you. At every twist and turn you were struck by the stark contrast between beauty and deprivation. The beauty of the nature and the people versus the harshness of the existence. We passed tea and banana plantations, went up and down hills and across plains and rivers. We saw some wild animals (zebra and antelope). Watching the people, however, hinted at the flipside of life, and they were everywhere. At no point did the road not have someone walking along it. The tall beautiful women in colourful dresses appealed to the classic romantic African fantasy until you saw just how weighty that basket of produce was on their heads. Children lugging heavy jerrycans of water. Men pushing rickety old bicycles laden with bananas, or fish, or bricks – anything that could be sold or used. There were numerous stalls offering fruit and vegetables and sometimes meat, and often women sitting on the earthen ground with a few pineapples on a towel in front of them hoping for a sale. Hand-to-mouth wasn't just an expression here, it was reality. And for every mile we covered we were followed by curious eyes, enthusiastic waves and shouted greetings from children. We were marked out by our colour.

Late morning the road crossed over the Equator and we entered the southern hemisphere, where we would remain until the return journey. We couldn't resist the opportunity to stop and take photos of ourselves under the "Equator" sign and with our feet in both hemispheres at the same time. Hours later we had lunch in the city of Mbarara, a welcome break from the bumpy backseat. As ever, I was drawn to people watching and taking in the surroundings.

At a table not far from us was a family with a woman holding a very fresh baby in her arms. This baby was so beautiful, huge dark eyes in a perfect dark face, I couldn't help but smile at the mother in acknowledgement. And then something extraordinary happened. She got up and brought the baby over to us, handing me the child so I could admire it more closely and have a cuddle. She was clearly proud of her new baby girl. She returned to her table while I cradled this gorgeous little being for a few minutes, deeply touched by the mother's gesture of sharing the joy of new life with a complete stranger. I then walked back to them and handed the baby back. During this whole interaction, not a single word was uttered between us mothers. We simply communicated through the *knowing*.

Our exhaustion gave way to elation as just before sunset we arrived at our destination and a view so breath-taking it was hard to fathom. The lodge was perched on top of a ridge overlooking the place where the Kazinga Channel converged into Lake Edward. From this peninsula you could see the stunning Rwenzori Mountains across the water with the Congo on the other side. We were just in time to see the sun turn into an enormous red ball before accelerating towards the edge of the horizon and disappearing below it. At the Equator, the sunset seemed to happen more quickly than in the north, I thought, because all at once we were enveloped in darkness.

We enjoyed these restful days which were an opportunity to process and assimilate the countless impressions we had had since our arrival. A much-needed pause. Unfortunately, we were all struggling with side effects of the anti-malarials by this time, ranging from gut issues and nausea to insomnia and headaches. Hamish assured Karina and I that this was nothing compared to having malaria so we just had to man up. Nonetheless, we managed some safari drives and a boat trip, excited to see sea eagles, lions, waterbucks and baboons amongst other animals. We were particularly amused by the free-roaming warthogs and mongoose who were allowed inside the lodge compound. You'd step out of your door and straight into the path of a line of warthog babies! Throughout, I was aware how the wildness of this nature was freeing up my heart, like I could breathe a little more easily into the heart space that was being created.

The day dawned for the return journey and we braced ourselves for the 286-mile return. At least we were taking the northern loop back to Kampala so we could see some more scenery. This included a stunning lake in a volcanic crater but best of all was the viewpoint overlooking The Great Rift Valley. It was simply awesome, this vast golden plain dotted with the iconic flat-topped acacia trees across the grassland. Geographically, it stretched south to Tanzania and north all the way to Djibouti through Ethiopia, as a group of independent interior basins. The valley basin in front of us was along the western edge. But the real significance for me was the fact we were standing on the cradle of civilisation, the very place where human life began two million years ago. Feeling the contact with this ancient red earth through my feet, I sensed a profound grounding. I grew roots as I stood. There was no *time* here, actual time was meaningless. Time was eternal. I realised in this moment that I wasn't "hanging out there". Instead I was profoundly connected to this Earth and to the human story.

Back in Jinja, Hamish and I packed up to fly home while Karina planned to stay for a few weeks to do charity work. We were a bit concerned with the political situation but Godfrey assured us it would be okay. As the plane lifted off the runway, skimming over the waves of Lake Victoria and the heads of the local fishermen in their wooden canoes before turning due north, I knew one thing. I would be back. My broken heart had found solace and healing in the heart of Africa, and in the process I had begun to find a way back to *myself*.

Arriving in West Sussex was awful. A kind of reverse culture shock. Everything seemed flat and colourless. Where was the *life*? The vibrancy? The energy? The streets were lined with parked cars, not people. Our local town had an abandoned feel to it, everyone minding their own business. I resented anything that sounded like a moan or complaint. Or entitlement, oh my god yes, *entitlement*. I couldn't bear that. I suffered waves of anger and rage mixed with sadness and longing, symptoms of "Africa withdrawal". I couldn't bring myself to go into the supermarket for a week. I eventually clicked back into First World rhythm but my mind kept drifting back to Uganda.

"We should do something, you know, support the charity more directly, not just send money," I said to Hamish over a cup of tea one afternoon. "When you think about it, it's skills and knowledge they need, not just cash."

"What could we do?"

"Well, surely there is something useful we can offer the projects JET is involved with. We're not teachers, so we couldn't do volunteer work in that way. But how about medical? You're a doctor, yeah?" I really did want to go back to Jinja.

"It's been a while since I worked in clinical practice."

"I know, but we could do something around health. You could do basic health checks for the children in the three orphanages and listen to what the aunties need to improve everyone's physical wellbeing." Images of the children we'd seen suffering long-term effects of malnourishment came into my head. Slow physical growth, high frequency of illness compared to other children, learning impairment.

"Yes, that sounds possible, good idea."

"Great! Leave it with me."

The plan to monitor the health of the JET children regularly and supply the orphanages with useful items like vitamins and protein supplements proved successful. It complemented the educational focus of the charity. After all, sick children don't go to school, do they? We had found a lovely quiet guest house to stay in where we got to know the staff. Arriving there felt like coming home to me, my heart opening a little more each time.

We would fly out to Uganda three more times, including a trip with Karina and her boyfriend during which they both did some volunteer teaching, before being grounded by the Covid pandemic. Although we initially went to "follow the money", I shall always be grateful to the people and country of Uganda for what they gave to me, more than words can really say and more than they will ever know.

Those who possess this [knowledge of the Self within] have equal regard for all.
They see the same Self in a spiritual aspirant and an outcaste, in an elephant, a cow, and a dog.
Bhagavad Gita 5.18

Chapter 5: Dog is God spelled backwards

"You should get a dog," said Joanna, "you'd love it."

"A dog? No way, Joanna, you've got to be joking! I'm a cat person."

"No, really, I think it would be good for you."

I had just wound up the school counselling service and it was mid-summer 2015. I was beginning to get comfortable with the idea of letting go and seeing what would come my way. And anyway it was true, I was a cat person, always have been. But a couple of years earlier, my cat days had come to a horrible end as the two young cats we had, brother and sister, both got killed on the busy road near our house just six months apart. It had been a cruel heartbreak on top of the still raw loss of Francesca. So I decided no more cats, it was too risky with that road, and my heart was not up for more pain.

But a dog? Wasn't that more responsibility? It would need to be trained and everything...

I mulled it over, though. Joanna knew me so well, I felt it wise to consider anything she suggested. I had the time, and logistically the house and garden had ample space for a larger pet. Perhaps a dog would be a good companion for me, would fill a growing emotional emptiness that I had become aware of?

We came up with the perfect solution. She was soon going on holiday for a week and I offered to look after her two dogs to see how I got on. Molly was a large Labradoodle reaching above my knee, all legs and shiny black poodle coat. Scruffy was a little guy, a Jackapoo with wiry sticky-up fur, he certainly lived up to his name. Little and large – I'd find out what size I preferred!

It turned out I did indeed love it. I laughed more that week than I had in ages. The joy! The playfulness! The lightness! They were one big ball of 24/7 positive energy. And after seven days of twice daily walks come rain or shine I felt really energised, fit and well. Indeed, by the time Joanna came back to collect them I looked like I had been the one away on holiday.

After the dogsitting I knew I wanted a large dog and a poodle mix. The combination of poodle smartness with Labrador sociability was appealing. A quick search on the internet and I found The Labradoodle Association, a self-regulated organisation with whom you could register litters if you met the requirements, e.g. health certificates, lineage, etc. I liked that idea because I didn't want to get a dog from some awful puppy farm. I could see there was a litter of Goldendoodles, Standard Poodle-Golden Retriever cross, due in September, which meant getting the puppy in November. Perfect, time to settle in just before Christmas. I contacted the breeder and completed the forms. I was clear I wanted a bitch as this was my first dog and females could be easier to handle and gentler in nature. I had discussed it with Joanna who had given this advice on the back of her long experience of both sexes. I told the breeder I was completely flexible and could come at any time to choose a puppy when the time came. I wanted to be sure and get the right one.

By now Karina and Hamish were fully on board with the upcoming arrival of a new family member. He had never had a pet in his life until we got the cats. We were all excited about the prospect of entering the canine world. However, it was clear this was to be my project. Karina was living at home at this time but was completing her second year of teacher training having graduated from university the year before. Hamish was away during the week working in London as usual.

I awaited the call from the breeder at around the time the puppies were old enough to be viewed, but in the end I called to make the appointment as I'd not heard anything. The three of us could hardly contain ourselves on the journey up to Oxford. For me, it felt a bit like heading for hospital with regular contractions to give birth! We discussed possible names. I quite liked Daisy.

We arrived full of expectation and got out of the car to meet the lady walking towards us on the driveway. She looked friendly and welcoming.

"Come this way," she said, pointing to a separate building to the house, "the puppies are kept in here." We entered a cosy annexe to a garage.

"I'm afraid there are only two puppies left. Two boys."

The three of us simultaneously froze and looked at each other.

"I'm sorry?" was all I managed to say.

"Yes, I had quite the response and when people came they chose one straight away!" It was her first go at breeding, her first litter. There had been nine puppies, five females and four males. Two of the females were to stay with the family and the other three had already been reserved.

In that moment I thought I would explode, the disappointment was so acute. What the hell had happened? I felt I had been *really very clear* about getting a female and that I could come whenever required to choose one. I was so angry I could hardly speak.

I kept my voice even as I said, "I was expecting to choose a female actually. I thought we had agreed."

If she realised the error, she didn't show it. A slight awkward pause followed.

"Okay, well, let's have a look at these two then," I eventually said.

She picked them up and we followed her back out and to the house in silence. While she busied herself making us a cup of tea in the kitchen, the three of us had a brief moment to ourselves.

"How did this happen?" asked Karina.

"No idea. But it is what it is. It's just really important that we don't take a puppy just because we're here. It needs to feel right, yeah? So let's not rush, let's each of us check them and then we'll see." They both agreed.

We turned our attention to the two little guys in the pen on the floor. They were beautiful and totally adorable, no question about that. It was our collective first time holding such a young puppy, they were only four weeks old. I quickly sensed one was more aloof and didn't like being handled and felt drawn to the other little chap. He seemed relaxed, interested and engaged. Each of us held him and he was not fussed. It was a big moment. It was not what I had wanted but... Perhaps it was meant to be like this? In the end we decided we honestly liked this puppy and decided to have him, collection in four weeks. A leap of faith.

One month later we were back and drove home with the new family addition. We had decided to call him Barley for his golden colouring – he was a quarter poodle and three quarters Golden Retriever. While we were waiting for collection day, I had thrown myself into puppy preparation and done research into dog training. I had bought and read one book in particular called *The Art of Raising a Puppy* by the Monks of New Skete. It had been recommended to me by a contact in America with lots of dog experience. I made notes and felt ready to implement the programme. How hard could it be?

Well, within days our lives descended into complete chaos as it became clear we had no idea what we were doing and the puppy was a nightmare. He seemed to want to bite and nip all the time, you could hardly get near him. I tried some training suggestions but they didn't work. For example, squealing loudly whenever he nipped me to warn him, but he just thought that was a game and nipped me more. With razor-sharp teeth. The other advice was to ignore the puppy when it was misbehaving. This resulted in Hamish having several pairs of pyjamas shredded as Barley jumped up to hang off the back of his legs as he walked away doing the "ignoring". I was stupid enough to wear my really nice and expensive goose down coat when trying this technique. It was too late as I heard the sound of tearing material as Barley's razor teeth made neat vertical incisions along the hem. I was really angry about that and the cost of having it mended.

Cuddles were far and few between, it was more like wrestling with a wild animal. What happened to the cuddly puppy fantasy? To all those cute puppy moments you'd see in magazines that I had been looking forward to? The evenings were the worst, Barley had to be quarantined in the kitchen where we took turns trying desperately to wear him out because he wouldn't settle. My resentment grew. I was meant to have had a gentle female after all and had been short-changed.

After a few weeks of being terrorised and crying a lot of the time, I called the breeder and said it was not working out, I wanted to give him back. It had been a mistake. Credit to her, she was supportive and reassuring, saying she was sure this was the right match. She asked what the issues were.

"The main problem is we don't have evenings anymore because he runs riot in the sitting room and one of us has to stay in the kitchen with him trying to tire him out."

"Tie him to the coffee table and distract him with chewy toys until he settles."

I hadn't thought of that. I could give it another go, knowing that at the end of the day I could always return him. At least in this way it was not like having a baby. The tying-up trick did make a difference but I was still struggling to get the situation under control. The fact was I found the whole thing utterly exhausting. There was no down-time in that I was aware of him and dealing with his needs every minute of the day, from the moment I woke up to going to bed. He was very good in some respects, though, we rarely had mishaps in the house and he had slept through the night no trouble from the very first night. It was the emotional and mental requirement on my part. I was used to cats, remember, super independent and self-sufficient. Barley was more like a child, he was completely dependent and needy. But the strength of my reaction indicated there was something else going on. Why was I failing? Why couldn't I manage this?

Luckily, some local friends of mine have a daughter who is a qualified dog trainer so I called them in desperation and asked for help. This family had a dog and a long history of dog ownership. So I turned up at their house one late afternoon a complete emotional and mental wreck after another harrowing day with Barley.

The moment we walked in they engaged with Barley. The husband was immediately delighted, lying straight down on the floor and rolling playfully around with him before I'd even taken off my coat. They were so confident and relaxed, I realised how fearful and tense I was. I sat on their sofa clutching a cup of tea and trying not to cry. I wished I could share their enthusiasm. What was wrong with me? The daughter arrived and showed me what to do when Barley got too bitey. Their much older and massive, dominant male Doberman-German Shepherd cross put Barley in his place too. I realised I needed to be the alpha in "the pack" because Barley had been allowed to think he was. And my family needed to help with showing him he was at the bottom of our hierarchy.

It was a turning point. I stepped up my training efforts and in doing so realised I had waited too long to train him, he was so smart. The books had all said start at 12 weeks but he had been ready the moment he arrived at our house at eight weeks. The nearest available puppy training class didn't start until he was 16 weeks. Part of the problem had been boredom.

Slowly I opened up to this extraordinary sentient Being and understood what that "something else" had been. I had been afraid to love Barley. I had not been prepared for how deeply he would touch my fragile and broken heart and I had been fighting it. He required *all my love*, not just a little. He required it *all the time*, not sometimes. He had reminded me too much of another small totally dependent being. Of Francesca. And subconsciously I was resisting bonding with him like I had with her in the early days, when I thought she was going to die. The fear was of making myself vulnerable again, of loving and therefore risking exposure to unbearable pain in the event of loss. Barley demanded that I open up my heart *more*. I had to commit to loving this dog fully, nothing less would do.

I needed to address this issue and try to get past it. I loosened the grip around my heart and approached Barley with enthusiasm and confidence like my friends. Everything shifted. He calmed down and all the lightness and joy I had imagined became real. He opened up the world of "dog owner" which transformed my life completely on many levels. The most obvious change was my physical fitness. I could feel the benefit of fresh air twice daily in all weathers. I had heard that having a dog boosts your immune system and could confidently confirm this fact. No more tedious frequent colds, I didn't fall ill at all during that winter. Having to find dog walks also expanded our knowledge of the local area. I'd lived here for years but been unaware of the beautiful environment so close to home. What joy to wander around the various nature reserves and discover wildlife and stunning scenery.

Barley also filled that emotional gap I had been feeling at home. By now Karina had completed her teacher training and moved to Bristol to be with her boyfriend and work there. I was alone most of the week but not at all lonely. Barley was my constant companion, "my guy". Whenever I needed a cuddle or affection I would simply throw myself onto the floor and roll around with him, kissing him as much as I wanted. He was always up for a love-in. I felt he had my back, had my interests at heart. He turned out to manifest that strong poodle protectiveness. If he felt he needed to warn me of something or someone, he'd give a proper deep bark. For example, he was not keen on seeing single men walking without dogs in the woods and would fire off a bark. One time, I was sitting quietly at the kitchen table when he suddenly barked really loudly, causing me to levitate off the chair. I looked around to see what had triggered him and saw through the window a huge hot air balloon hovering very close to the house. Barley had felt that was not normal, it wasn't supposed to be there, so a warning was in order.

The most telling example of how smart Barley was, though, happened one night. I had settled him down and gone upstairs, turning out the light to sleep. Suddenly I heard one bark, not a loud one, so much so that I wasn't sure whether I'd heard it at all. Silence. Then another bark, just one, same tone. Oh bugger, I was all settled in bed and didn't feel like waking myself up going downstairs. It hadn't sounded urgent. Okay, if he barked one more time I'd go and investigate. Silence. I went to sleep. Next morning, I went downstairs to discover that I had left all the lights on in the kitchen! Poor Barley had spent the whole night fully flood-lit. He looked bleary-eyed and annoyed. What a clever dog. I never ignored his warning bark again.

Hamish enjoyed the dog as well when he was at home. He confessed to having wanted a male dog all along, perhaps to balance out the mother-daughter female axis. I could understand that actually. Barley brought out the playful side of him and it was good for us to have a common focus of interest, something we could share. However, I noticed he kept using different words as commands to those I was training the dog with, even after I'd point it out. After all my efforts, I didn't want him to confuse Barley, we needed to be consistent so the training could be reinforced. I couldn't understand why this was hard. But I need not have feared, Barley was so intelligent he seemed to be bilingual in any case.

Then there was the unexpected upside of the social aspect of dog ownership. I could talk to people, to complete strangers, without feeling weird. Having a dog gave you permission to chat to anyone, whether they had a dog or not. This was a revelation to me as I was one of those people who always kept to themselves when out and about. I tended to avoid casual conversing, just wanting to get on with my business. Now, I took the time to notice and engage with fellow humans and their four-legged friends. It turned out most dog owners are nice friendly people, so I allowed myself to open up a little more. Another upside was that you could talk to yourself out loud, and if you met someone, you could always say you were talking to the dog.

One fine morning on a dog walk, I came towards a clearing in the woods when a woman stepped into the shaft of light and stopped to look at me. She had a little terrier-type dog with her. We greeted each other and started to chat about our dogs, as you do. Her name was Sarah and the dog was called Bertie. I became immediately aware of her positive energy, and we struck up an instant rapport. Our dogs also hit it off which was another sign we were destined to be friends.

It was uncanny how much common ground we had. She was also a counsellor. She had been born abroad, in Hong Kong. Her family story, like mine, was complicated and included painful upheavals like parental divorce and difficult family dynamics. There was lots to talk about. With the confidence I had gained from my friendship with Joanna I felt able to trust and lean in. She lived just minutes away and turned out to run her own healing product business. The usefulness of this goes without saying! We exchanged numbers and soon fell into a routine of meeting regularly for walks.

One of the things I was still battling with was Barley's diet. From the beginning he had gut issues, ranging from colitis to bile vomiting. I tried everything – raw protein, cooked protein, all kinds of kibble. He just didn't settle down. I researched it and discovered that food sensitivity was not uncommon in Golden Retrievers. I sought advice from the vet but made little progress. I felt I was going around in circles.

On a walk with Sarah I started to cry, the whole thing had just got to me. I wanted to nurture this animal and my efforts were being constantly rejected.

"It's like Francesca all over again! I couldn't feed her either and she was always ill. No matter how hard I tried I couldn't turn it around."

Sarah knew about the Francesca story and understood why I linked it in this way to Barley. I knew why I was upset too. It was my profound fear of loss and pain resurfacing. Others would probably not react like this and simply take the problem in their stride without all the emotion.

"Look, Mina, why don't you throw Barley back into the universe?"

"What?"

"Let him go and let the universe decide. You can't go on living in fear. You are not in control and this clinging will get you nowhere."

"How do I do that?"

"Release the reins and trust."

Although the tears kept coming I instinctively knew what she meant. Loving someone, or a sentient being like a dog, is an act of letting go, isn't it? It's ultimately an act of faith because you don't *own* that being. You don't control the life of him/her/it. Bad things can happen to those we care about at any time, that's life. There is nothing to be gained by constantly anticipating it, though. Lots of people do this in relationships of course, but only because they come from a place of insecurity. It's fear again, fear of pain. And what it brings is unhappiness, no surprise there. A constant sense of uneasiness and tension which can be entirely unconscious. Only to surface when the dog you have allowed into your fragile heart is vomiting up the goodness, the love, you're trying to give it. In the words of Sting, *if you love someone, set them free*. Indeed.

Easier said than done, however, and it doesn't happen overnight. I was disappointed with myself in a way because after all the spiritual work with Colin, which had come to a close three years earlier, you would think I would be at peace. That by understanding the big spiritual picture I had arrived at acceptance. But clearly there was some kind of significant residue left that needed to be dealt with.

Eventually I did find a diet that worked for Barley, it turned out he is highly allergic to protein. He is now fit and well. Thank you, universe, for the opportunity to work out some more of my stuff. However, I continued to think seriously about this connection with the cosmos, specifically through my relationship with Barley. The love between man and dog has been present for millennia and is well documented. But why is it special? Because they give you the very things we sometimes lack in our human life, that we fail to give to each other: unconditional love, trust and joy. They accept you as you are, warts and all, with no judgement. Their hearts are open (only closing when they are mistreated). We simply need to treat them with a little kindness and respect and they will keep on giving.

Well, the whole unconditional-love-trust-and-joy thing hadn't really worked out for me so far, to be honest. I still felt life had not been very nice to me at all. Yes, I had spiritually grown with Colin. Yes, I had begun the heart opening with Joanna and now Barley. Could I suddenly believe everything was going to be all right going forward and the universe was directing me to some cool new place?

Some time later, Sarah sent me a link to a video on YouTube. It was about a stallion called Peyo who worked as a therapy horse. His handler would take him regularly into this particular hospital where he was allowed to wander around and choose which patient room he wanted to enter. He was never led in any way, he always chose who he wanted to see, as if knowing where he was needed. The joy on people's faces was clear as he lifted away their worries and pain for a few moments, nuzzling them with his soft muzzle.

The camera followed him choosing to go into a room where a young man lay dying, we know not of what but that didn't matter. The man was tired and haggard and clearly physically weak. Peyo stepped right up to him and brought his huge head level with his face. Their eyes met as the young man was drawn into the horse's gaze. Suddenly he burst into tears. At first I wasn't sure what just happened but now I think I know why he was crying. Peyo's enormous brown soulful eyes were showing him the universe, showing him unconditional love, trust and joy. He was being shown the Source. He was being shown the *return*. And it was not frightening at all, in fact, it was quite beautiful and the young man was going to be okay.

When Francesca died something in me died too. I disconnected and became separate in my pain. I now needed to find my way back. I needed to throw *myself* back into the universe, and Barley could be my guide and mentor. He was the right dog for me after all. He could be my canine, not equine, healing therapist. Whenever I looked into his eyes, I would always see those three things there: love, trust and joy. That is the gift all animals offer us all the time if we just bother to look – the direct connection to Source through their eyes. And that is why dog is God spelled backwards.

So, the time with Colin had helped me understand the spiritual world intellectually and Barley was encouraging me to believe it. But could this lovely dog continue to fill the growing void I mentioned earlier? Because it felt like the more I opened up my heart, the larger the emptiness became. I sensed the presence of anger and resentment lurking in the depths. What was the connection I was missing?

*Cut through this doubt in your own heart with the
sword of spiritual freedom.
Arise; take up the path of yoga!
Bhagavad Gita 4.42*

Chapter 6: It's only a matter of time until the mat becomes the altar

"You all right there? That seemed like a big movement."

Debs, the yoga teacher, had looked over in my direction having heard a loud crack. I was lying face up on a yoga mat staring at the ceiling and wondering what the hell had just happened. I had heard it too, obviously.

"Yeah, all good here, thanks," I replied, feeling a bit embarrassed. The other students had looked towards me as well.

It was my first yoga class and to start with we had simply been asked to lie down in *savasana* (Corpse Pose) and relax. But when I had stretched out my legs and let go of all the muscular tension, the weight of my body and the pull of gravity had realigned my pelvis. My right hip had released and dropped about half an inch, hence the sound.

I have to back up a bit here. This was the summer of 2011 and I had just completed my counselling training, four years before losing my job and getting Barley. Hamish and I had got married in late spring. I had come back from honeymoon with excruciating back pain that had started the day we were returning home. It felt like being stabbed with a knife in my lower right sacro-iliac joint. I hadn't experienced this before. I immediately sought out chiropractor treatment, and for a couple of months I spent a lot of money not getting any better. One day I happened to flick through the local parish newsletter and saw an advert for yoga classes in the village hall not far from me. On an impulse I decided to go. I knew nothing about yoga but had nothing to lose.

So there I was on the floor, already feeling relief. My joy was short-lived, however, as we worked through the yoga sequence. Oh my goodness, my body was in such a state. I managed to lift my tailbone into Downface Dog for a nanosecond before my arms gave out, my whole body shaking like jelly. I couldn't breathe, sweat pouring off my face. I tried to lean back into a gentle backbend. I couldn't breathe, sweat pouring off my face. I could hardly do anything, I couldn't bend in any direction, not forwards, not backwards. Every muscle was weak. And hurt. I had neither strength nor flexibility anywhere.

I left the class feeling upset and horrified. I had no idea my state of fitness was that bad but I knew how I had arrived here. When Francesca had been alive there had been no opportunity for "me-time", as I was either working in London during the week or at home looking after the girls and keeping the house sorted at the weekends. Going to a gym would have been too indulgent, selfish even. After she died, I guess I had no interest. I had the time but no inclination. In any case, that yoga class was a major wake-up call and I made a commitment there and then to continue with yoga and sort myself out.

My yoga story then developed into two parallel paths, physical and spiritual, with Debs as my guide to start with. We became friends and embarked on a joint exploration of different yoga approaches. On the physical level, as the weeks and months passed, my body gradually softened, stretched and strengthened. Patience was key, this was going to be a long-term project, clearly.

I attended Debs' classical Hatha yoga classes every week, but at the same time we decided to try other yoga styles to see what we could learn. I had been to a few classes in London taught by Bridget Woods-Kramer of Anusara yoga and brought Debs with me there one time. Developed by John Friend, this was a form of Hatha yoga emphasising alignment, specifically the three A's of Attitude, Alignment and Action. The concept of spirals and loops bringing balance to each pose.

We went to a Scaravelli-inspired yoga workshop run by Christine Borg. Here the emphasis was on awakening the spine, approaching yoga as an experience, not a pose. More feeling your way into the yoga *asana* (Sanskrit for the physical practice of yoga poses) rather than applying a method. I went on my first solo residential retreat, a weekend with Simon Low practising his yin-yang offering. This was my first foray into restorative (yin) yoga where we held poses for longer supported by props. The yang sequences were stronger and exertive. Debs and I went to a workshop run by Jenny Beeken, author of several books on the various physical and spiritual healing aspects of yoga. We drove to Brighton and met Peter Blackaby, learning about his "intelligent yoga" which focused on the functional aspect of the body, "the nervous system, body mapping and innate intelligence of the body". There was always something new to learn and consider, and it was fun to have Debs to discuss it with.

I noticed that some of these teachers had trained with BKS Iyengar in India and, becoming curious, decided to do my own reading about the origins of modern yoga. I was surprised to find that the physical practice of yoga as we know it today is relatively new. The "father of modern yoga" was Tirumalai Krishnamacharya (1888-1989), widely regarded as the most influential yoga teacher in the 20th century and responsible for reviving Hatha yoga. He was also an ayurvedic healer. He must have been onto something, living to the ripe old age of 100 years. Anyway, he developed the notion of combining breathing with movement, working with yoga postures to promote health and wellbeing. His students include renowned and influential yoga teachers such as BKS Iyengar (1918-2014), K Pattabhi Jois (1915-2009), and his own son DKV

Desikachar (1938-2016), all of whom founded their own yoga schools. Iyengar yoga takes classical Hatha yoga and works with alignment and props. Pattabhi Jois founded Ashtanga yoga (linking yoga postures with flowing movement, called vinyasa), and his son developed a style called Viniyoga.

Looking at these past and current yoga teachers, it became clear to me that each one took something from the "Hatha yoga pot" and developed their own personal offering. I thought that was very beautiful. It was also inspiring – learning could never end! You would never arrive, as it were, you just kept growing as yoga kept giving. I learned something new about the body with each offering, either through direct teaching or a book, and applied what I needed to my own practice. My go-to friends for all things yoga body became *The Path to Holistic Health* by BKS Iyengar, *The Key Poses of Yoga* by Ray Long, *Hatha Yoga Pradipika* by Swami Muktibodhananda and *Yoga Anatomy* by Leslie Kaminoff & Amy Matthews. My body awareness grew along with my strength.

Debs also opened the door to the spiritual side of yoga. This aspect interested me because it tied in with the spiritual philosophy exploration I had shared with Colin. I had thoroughly enjoyed reading about medieval and European spirituality, but I felt there was more I could learn now that the journey with Colin was coming to an end. It looked like fate had directed my spiritual quest further east, to the ancient yogic scriptures of India. Debs recommended a book to get started.

And so it was that in the summer of 2013, two years after lying down on the yoga mat for the first time, I found myself turning to the first page of *Yoga and the Quest for the True Self* by Stephen Cope. And finding the title for this chapter! This book provided the first opportunity to sense check where I was at in my body as well as in my heart. It made me reflect on my life so far and how I had arrived here. I thought about my survival strategy to date, being strong and capable outside to protect the soft injured inside, tying in with what I had learned from Joanna. I thought about how I carried my disappointment, this heavy load for my body and soul. I reviewed my physical state and was reminded of the need to relax and *breathe*.

The book also introduced me to some key yogic tenets, the five afflictions (*kleshas*) of the human state:

Avidya – ignorance
Asmita – I-ness
Raga – attraction
Dvesha – aversion
Abhinivesha – clinging to life and death

and the four erroneous beliefs that sustain the *kleshas*:

The belief in the permanence of objects
The belief in the ultimate reality of the body
The belief that our state of suffering is really happiness
The belief that our bodies, minds and feelings are our true Self

This was quite the mouthful but I understood the underlying message: stop looking "out there" and start looking "in here". Cope referred to the Wizard of Oz to make the point, where Dorothy says at the end of the movie when she finds herself back in Kansas, "Now I realise it was all *right here* to begin with". He sums it up by writing, "our desire for life to be the way we want it to be, rather than the way it is, is finally what chains us to the great wheel of karma, the wheel of suffering, that goes round and round through endless eons". Sounded like it was time to get off it then.

To get a better understanding of what a "yogi" is, what a person who practises yoga on all levels is actually like, I then read *Autobiography of a Yogi* by Paramahansa Yogananda (1893-1952), founder of the Self-Realisation Fellowship. What an incredible life he led. I had no idea up to that point the breadth and depth of yoga and the profound effect it can have on a human being with dedicated practice.

Curious and ready to go further into the yogic philosophy literature, the next book I read was *The Essence of the Bhagavad Gita* by Eknath Easwaran. This was an eye opener. Many interpretations and translations have been written about the *Bhagavad Gita* of course, but Easwaran explains the key yogic themes clearly and beautifully. As I explain at the beginning of the book, this is one of the key ancient texts that offers a way to live a fulfilled life in the yogic tradition.

What was particularly helpful with this book was how it enabled me to come to an even more comfortable place with Francesca's death from where I had got to with Colin. In the second chapter, Sri Krishna says to Arjuna:

Death is inevitable for the living; birth is inevitable for the dead. Since these are unavoidable, you should not sorrow." (BG: 2.27).

Then shortly after, he adds:

The Self of all beings, living within the body, is eternal and cannot be harmed. Therefore, do not grieve." (BG: 2.30).

What I think this means is that the universe is everything and everything is the universe. Human beings are manifestations of the universe, in the physical form of specific atoms and molecules which we know all about scientifically, along with every other living creature and thing on this planet we call Earth. A rock, tree, lion and person simply display a different combination of universal matter. All other planets and stars also manifest the universe, however numerous, including whatever exists there. Therefore, each and every one of us carries the essence of the universe in us. Death is a return to this essence, not a complete disappearance. Our time here is a passing-through in this particular dimension. Some things exist for a very long time, like a rock or a tree, or a planet. Other things only have days or weeks, like insects. The same applies to humans – some live to be very old, some only hours. Francesca had just over twelve years. But however long you are here, you're still made up of the universe.

Well, how exciting was this? I of course recognised my old friends Plotinus and Eriugena here. The message about our connection and return to the One, the Source, was the same but in much older texts. It was too similar to be coincidental and I wondered whether they had come across the yogic scriptures in their lifetimes. I contacted Colin to ask him. Yes, that could indeed have been the case, he said. Spiritual teachings from India had travelled West along the trading routes and been spread amongst the thinking communities.

I recalled how Colin and I had discussed this essence we all have that can be called Soul, or Self, or God, or the One. It doesn't really matter what name you give it. It doesn't even matter if you don't acknowledge it, it's still there. The new line of thought, the new angle that the *Bhagavad Gita* was offering to me was not about where do we come from and where do we go, or how long have we got here (although these questions are addressed in the story). The really important question is ***how will I live my life while I have it***, while I'm manifesting this particular human physical form of the universe?

It turned out Eastern philosophy has a lot to say about that. All the key texts converge on the same point: our purpose in this life is to realise our True Self. The *Bhagavad Gita* shows us that we have come into life to learn that nothing finite can satisfy. If we all have the essence of the universe inside us, wouldn't it be great to actually connect to it? Consciously? To feel and tap into this eternal power, nurturing and strength? To lean into a deep and unwavering sense of belonging and groundedness? And do it *now*, today and every day.

Well, we can. Every human being can do it. But there are some things that stand in our way that we must overcome, and that's where the challenge lies. First of all, we must let go of the Ego. This is no easy feat because the Ego is incredibly strong. It controls us through our senses, our desires and our mind. It tells us we need to buy more stuff to be happy. That we need to have cosmetic surgery, live in a bigger house, earn more money, have higher status, have cooler friends, have bigger muscles, have more sex, go for more fancy holidays etc., etc., to be happy. All these desires keep us in a state of separateness, in a state of continuous and uninterrupted "I" vs "them".

This is a very stressy state of being and living, as we all know. Everybody is so bloody stressed and worn out with the constant striving, grasping, clinging to more and more and more. It's silly because we never get there, of course, moments of satisfaction and fulfilment are fleeting before we're on to the next thing. The Ego tells us it's never enough because it doesn't want to lose control. And then what happens? We **suffer**. We sit with the pain of failure and dissatisfaction. It doesn't have to be dramatic, perhaps a niggling discomfort in the back of the mind that you can't seem to shake off completely.

Therefore, we need to wean ourselves off our dependence on the Ego. All the sensory driven stuff is just noise distracting us from what really matters.

According to the yogic scriptures there are three attitudes, or *samskaras*, that keep us separate and in the suffering. *Samskaras* are the subtle impressions of our past actions. Each time the action is repeated, the impression becomes stronger and forms a habit, a pattern. Think of it like a mental track you begin walking on which becomes deeper and deeper the longer you walk over the same place until it feels more like a ditch or trench. Over time it gets so deep that you can't see over it, climb out of it or change direction.

The three big yogic *samskaras* are:

1. *Kama*: selfish desire/sensory craving
2. *Krodha*: anger
3. *Bhaya*: fear

If your prime motivation is, or if you lead with, one or more of these, life is going to be pretty shitty. It's going to be hard being stuck here. We can spend an awful long time and a lot of energy going around in circles with these three, all of which is just "junk food for the mind" (Eknath Easwaran) at the end of the day. And we get nowhere. And hurt ourselves and others in the process.

The second yogic piece of advice is we need to practise detachment. How do we do that? By not being attached to results. We seem to spend a lot of time focusing on and worrying about what will or won't happen next. Will I get that job? Pass that exam? Find the dream partner? Get pregnant? Find the perfect house? We also keep ourselves as the frame of reference, for example, always asking what are he/she/they doing or not doing for *me*? Again, this is very stressy! So try this: just throw your intention or wish out there and let the universe decide. This can be sending in a job application or going on a first date or starting a creative project. Don't be concerned about whether it will work out or not. Take a leaf out of Gandhi's book (he knew a thing or two about letting go of the Ego and finding his True Self) who said "Do your best, then leave the results to God". As I wrote in the previous chapter, I would later hear this sentiment expressed by Sarah when I was battling with my fear around Barley's health.

The third point, and related to detachment, is to live in the present moment. Yes, this is an oft-heard cliché I know, but the scriptures are clear about this. Living in the past or in the future is an illusion, it's not real. It's part of the Ego's game of keeping us wishing, wanting and yearning. The only reality is now.

I continued to read all manner of spiritual offerings and found the *Bhagavad Gita* reflected in them all. I checked in with Alan Watts' *The Wisdom of Insecurity* and *The Way of Zen*. I liked his reminder that change and death are life's necessary parts – to work for their exclusion is to work against life. I read the inspiring *Walking to the Mountain* by Wendy Teasdill, her amazing story of walking to, around and from Mount Kailash in Tibet on her own. Next up was *The Cloud of Unknowing*, a 14th century text written by an unknown person thought to be a priest from the East Midlands. He wrote:

For it is not what you are or have been that God looks at with his merciful eyes, but what you would be,

and

Strain every nerve in every possible way to know and experience yourself as you really are.

Two hundred years later in Spain St John of the Cross wrote a beautiful poem called *The Dark Night*, a description of what felt like his actual experience of meditating and uniting with God, with Source.

I then returned to India figuratively speaking and read *My Lord Loves a Pure Heart* by Swami Chidvilasananda, a modern day female yogi, which made a change. Inspired by the *Bhagavad Gita*, she offers nine key ingredients for having a good heart necessary to live a decent life: fearlessness, purity of being, steadfastness in yoga, steadfastness in knowledge, freedom from anger, compassion, humility, respect and selfless service. She brings the focus back to what she feels is the core of the matter, that to *love* is the supreme goal in life. She wrote that the one thing you never forget about someone who has died is your love for that person and that person's love for you. Well, I certainly knew that to be true with Francesca. But I especially liked her point that "a faint-hearted person always tries to bargain with life". Isn't that the truth? Wouldn't we all prefer to stay on the path of least resistance if it worked? If that actually solved our problems and made the tough stuff go away?

I dipped into *Living Dangerously* by Osho. As well as reminding me that living in the past and the future wastes the present, and that you must "squeeze the whole juice out of life", his nugget for me was the idea that if you have loved someone totally and they die, there is no wound left. Yes, that should be the case, shouldn't it? If you have given all your love to someone then there is no love lost. I found that reassuring but I guess the pain for me was the wish to give more, to keep loving Francesca.

Next, I enjoyed *The Anatomy of the Spirit* by Caroline Myss. She draws on seven sacred truths that the Hindu/*chakra*, Judaic Kabbalah and Christian sacraments share and that lie at the centre of our spiritual power. This approach affirmed my view that religions ultimately come from a common source: every human being is the essence of God (what I think of as the universe). Like the previous authors, she emphasises the importance of living in the moment and honouring oneself, that love is the divine power and All is One. Myss concludes that there are three threads common to the three spiritual traditions and they are worth including here:

1. Ignoring one's spirit will affect one's body and life.
2. Every person will encounter a series of challenges that will activate a crisis of faith: what/who do I have faith in?

3. To heal from a misdirected spirit, one must release the past and return to the present moment.

She adds that the physical world, our life in this dimension, serves the learning of our spirits.

This resonated with me hugely, I have to say, as I had experienced and was working through all three points. Fear had largely dictated my life until Francesca died and had had an effect on my body, as the yoga had showed me. The loss precipitated a spiritual crisis. And now I was in the healing process physically through the yoga and spiritually through the reading. Once again, I found reassurance, spurring me onwards.

In October 2016 I had an opportunity to attend a whole day workshop with Alan Shearer who had written his own interpretation of Patanjali's Yoga Sutras (*sutra* means rule or aphorism, a pithy observation that contains a general truth). It was an opportunity to immerse myself in this key yogic text. Patanjali lived in India 150-200 CE and was one of the first to write down and document the ancient learnings that had been passed down through time via the oral tradition. He described eight paths to enlightenment, to connection with your inner being or what I think of as our essence.

What I gleaned from the discussion was, don't expect one yogic text to give you the whole story. No, indeed! That was clear from my diverse book list. Also, he said we needed to transcend thinking, not think more. Yes, I heard that loud and clear, this warning, be wary of staying in your head. Easy to do with all this reading. But I especially liked his view that the (eight) limbs (of yoga) don't grow one after the other, sequentially, but rather in proportion. So if you think of a tree, it doesn't grow one branch individually until it's done and then another and another. It grows its branches upwards and outwards together, sprouting one here and then there, growing at different stages but finally all branches fully outstretched to reach its beautiful mature and proportional shape. I found this image helpful, the eight paths developing together:

Yamas (attitude to others)
Niyamas (attitude to oneself)
Asana (physical practice)
Pranayama (conscious breathing)
Pratyahara (steadying the mind, withdrawing the senses)
Dharana (intense focus, one-pointedness)
Dhyana (meditation)
Samadhi

Samadhi is where all roads lead, to self-realisation, to bliss (*ananda*), to union with God, to Oneness, to enlightenment, to merging with the universe, whatever you want to call it. Maybe we reach *samadhi* in this lifetime, maybe not. Listening to Alan Shearer I felt it would happen naturally when you were ready. It wouldn't work by going through this list and ticking them off one by one.

At this point I could see I had started to grow my branches, my most advanced being *asana* and *pranayama.* I had found meditating the most challenging and the other branches had not yet sprouted. It had been a most informative and enjoyable day.

My yogic literature library continued to grow. For a deep intellectual dive into the history of the yogic scriptures including the different kinds of yoga and the six schools of Hindu philosophy (of which yoga is one), I found the mighty *The Yoga Tradition* by Georg Feuerstein helpful. This book was so thorough (and big!) that I used it for dipping in and out. Other books I savoured were the *Shiva* and *Gheranda Samhitas* translated by James Mallinson, a second book by Swami Chidvilasananda, *The Yoga of Discipline*, *The Yoga Sutras of Patanjali* by Swami Satchidananda and the awesome *Inner Engineering* by Sadhguru.

Each tome I picked up offered me something, a little gift, a gold nugget, to add to the others that came before, until it felt like a basket of gold whose growing weight anchored me more and more into the earth. It was a waking up, an opening and expanding of my mind at the top and a grounding down at the bottom simultaneously.

Sitting with all these affirmations, this wisdom stretching back thousands of years, gave me rest. Life isn't a judgement, it just *is*. Life can be painful at times and the only way is through it. It was here I found the meaning I had been looking for in losing my child. Through her death I could learn to embrace life more fully. This felt more appropriate, made more sense to me, than putting my loss down to just bad luck. Or worse, as some sort of punishment. So, the good news was I had found my "spiritual home" in the Eastern scriptures. Reading was easy, but could I put it into practice? Could I let go of my Ego, for example? Could I detach? Step off that wheel of karma going round and round? Anyway, what was my ever-deepening mental track, my *samskara*?

I knew the answer to the last question. My lifelong *samskara* was deep resentment from ***not being heard***. During Francesca's life I had also lived in *bhaya* (fear), the third of the three big samskaras I described earlier. But now I was hooked on the second, on *krodha* (anger). A constant gnawing feeling of "it's not about me" but about everybody else. That I didn't matter. In counselling speak, it was my inner abandoned child crying out. When this was triggered in any situation, it caused me huge pain. This wound went a long way back, and I knew the origin through my own counselling therapy. But how not to take the bait when dangled in front of me in the moment and fall down into that trench? This, at the time, was less clear to me. I knew it intellectually but I didn't seem able to withstand the emotional pull. And that was the problem. Life with Barley and reading about the Eastern yogic scriptures were opportunities to effect real change, to a different way of being, but I was having trouble moving from thinking to behaving. To consciously living more spiritually and applying the yogic guidance. I was so comfortable staying in my head…

I had been practicing yoga and going to classes for five years when one day Debs suggested I should consider becoming a teacher myself. Me, a teacher? No way, you've got to be joking. I found the mere suggestion of it daunting, terrifying. But a seed had been sown and I played around with the concept in my mind. It wasn't that crazy a notion, after all, I come from a family of teachers. My paternal grandparents had had careers in education, as had my uncle and my aunt. My cousin was a teacher, and even my own daughter had recently qualified as a teacher! I had the time, I was in the enviable position of no work commitments. I could do yoga teacher training as part of personal development, as a life experience. It didn't have to be a means to an end with some sort of teaching commitment or plan at the end of it. Indeed, here was an opportunity to practise detachment and just throw it out there. Perhaps this was what would help me finally shift up into a higher spiritual gear.

As all yoga teachers know, there are a lot of yoga teacher training programmes to choose from. I was quite overwhelmed when I first started my online search. It was clear you could spend serious money without a guarantee of high quality and thorough instruction. It was very much buyer beware and diligence required. What I was sure of was that I wanted to immerse myself in yoga, to go somewhere and learn full time. Basically to eat, breathe, sleep and live yoga.

I eventually found a yoga school I resonated with, that had the right mix of practical and philosophic instruction. Yogic philosophy was important to me, obviously, and had to be part of the offering. Importantly, the school was registered with the Yoga Alliance. Yoga, like counselling, is not regulated, but there are organisations that regulate its members, so you know that a set of standards must be adhered to if affiliated with them. The Akasha Yoga Academy was founded and run by a German couple out of Bali and Thailand. Gosh, Southeast Asia, I had never been there before. That was very far from home. This was going to be way out of my comfort zone and I felt a bit scared. All that way, all on my own for a whole month. To be sure I was making the right choice I decided to accept the online offer of a Skype session. I was duly reassured after speaking with Burkhard, one of the founders. It felt like the right fit.

I called Hamish, who was in London for his usual work week there. I wondered what he'd say about such a crazy plan.

"I've decided I'd like to do yoga teacher training. It would mean I'd be away for a month though."

"What are the dates?"

"Sorry?" I thought he must have misheard me. There was no reaction in his voice of surprise or curiosity or even annoyance. I'd been expecting something like, "Wow, really? Where did that come from?", or "That sounds amazing, how exciting!" or "A month? How the hell do you expect me to work and look after the dog?" A normal reaction. I mean, a month is a long time to be apart, isn't it?

"I need to know the dates so I can plan for Board meetings."

"Oh, right."

I gave him the dates and that was the end of the conversation, he asked no more questions. I guessed it didn't matter. I duly fell into my *samskara*. Feeling a bit hurt and annoyed, I said to myself, "Well, I'll just go then!" I looked at the programme dates and chose the 4-week course for April 2017 the following year.

Oh my god, I'd done it, I'd paid my deposit. This was actually going to happen.

Now listen to the principles of yoga.
By practising these you can break through
the bonds of karma.
On this path effort never goes to waste,
and there is no failure.
Bhagavad Gita 2.39 and 2.40

Chapter 7: Bali

I looked down at the print on the boarding pass in my hand.

Flight CX252
from London Heathrow to Hong Kong
Date 23 Mar 2017, Boarding Time 10.45

It was hard to believe. The big day had finally arrived and there I was, standing in front of the entrance to the security check at Terminal 3 with a rucksack on my back, my yoga mat bag slung over one shoulder and a ticket for the Cathay Pacific flight to Hong Kong with a connection to Denpasar Airport in Bali. I was heading a scary 7,755 miles east. Excitement and fear coursed through my veins. I had never done anything as bold as this in my life. But it felt absolutely *right*. I needed to go and explore. To have a break from the daily routine. Since signing up to the course I had not been able to shake my feeling of being "stuck" in every way, no matter how many dog walks I took and yoga philosophy books I read. Boarding this flight felt empowering. I really wanted things to change. I sincerely hoped Bali would provide some answers, offer me solutions.

One thing was certain, I didn't need to deal with the grief and loss of Francesca on this trip. I had done the work and had left that behind me.

I felt well prepared for the yoga course. As soon as I had signed up, I had been sent a lot of pre-reading which I worked through during the seven months before going. Anatomy was a subject I knew the least about, so I focused on that. And on the philosophy, of course. I also received lots of support for all the logistics – accommodation, taxi pick-up at the airport etc. It was reassuring to know I would be met by someone. I had definitely chosen the right teacher training course, everything offered was thorough and well thought through. I could tell the instruction was going to be intense but that was exactly what I wanted. Live, eat, breathe yoga, that was the aim.

What I wasn't prepared for, however, was how it would feel to arrive in the jungle. Heat, yes, but not this level of humidity. I had been travelling for 21 hours and arrived in Ubud just before sunset. Ubud was inland and up into the hills, very different to the cooler coastal Bali climate. The drive from the airport had revealed beautiful architecture, elaborate wood carvings and lush greenery. The importance of religion to the Balinese was apparent in the many shrines we passed along the way. They worshipped their own version of Hinduism. The whole impression was of the exotic, I felt as if I was on a different planet but in a good way.

The taxi entered what looked like the beginning of the town's high street but we turned off up a dirt track which came to a dead end. The driver said I would have to get out here and walk the rest of the way to the place where the yoga training would take place and where I was staying. Thankfully he said he would carry my suitcase. I don't think I would have coped otherwise. My anxiety levels, already high, increased as we made our way along a cobbled dirt pathway that wound its way between low houses and rice paddy fields. The heat was intense, likewise the humidity. Sweat poured off my whole body. Didn't it cool down at the end of the day here?

Eventually we got to a large wooden gate on the left and the driver said we had arrived. I gave him a generous tip and felt sad to see his back disappear down the track. I had enjoyed his comforting company. There seemed to be no one around. Eventually I found a young man who hardly spoke any English. He got my name, though, and showed me to my bungalow. The accommodation was made up of a mixture of separate bungalows and rooms attached to other buildings. So, underneath the shala, the open-air yoga space which had a beautiful wooden roof, I could see two rooms. I had chosen a bungalow because I thought that would offer more privacy and be quieter.

I stood alone in a small bedroom of what was a simple wood structure perched on a slope backing onto a paddy field. It was more basic than I had expected but the view from the balcony facing the deep river valley was beautiful. Vast trees and shrubs with colourful flowers were everywhere. The only other door lead to a little ensuite bathroom. I was okay with everything really, but it was just so hot! Uncomfortably so. There was no cooling breeze coming from anywhere. The little fan attached high up on one wall offered no relief as it simply wafted the hot air in circles. I knew I would have to keep all doors and windows closed at night to keep out the many biting insects, so I would just have to get used to the heat.

As I was taking all this in, I will admit to losing my nerve slightly and wanting to cry. Today was Karina's 25th birthday and I was thousands of miles from home. I was going to live here for a month which felt like a very long time suddenly. I gave in to a few moments of doubt and self-pity before realising that panic was going to get me nowhere. I had to man up and get a grip. This had been my choice and I was responsible. I felt it would calm me down to unpack and get organised in the space. I was also hungry and would need to get something to eat before going to sleep. I knew from my travels in Africa that I mustn't forget to buy bottled water for drinking and brushing teeth and for that I needed to find a shop. There was nothing for it but to walk back to town and check out the scene.

Light was fading as I made my way down the high street. It was a bit overwhelming and my fatigue was getting to me now. I just wanted to find somewhere okay and safe to eat. Not knowing where to go made me anxious, I didn't want to pick up a tummy bug. I hate to admit this, but when I caught sight of the unmistakeable and reassuringly familiar Starbucks sign, I made a bee line for it. Inside, I could have been anywhere in the world. It was the same as the one I'd been to in Beijing, same as the countless outlets in California and England. Guilt and shame for not being more adventurous were quickly dispelled as I relaxed into the air conditioning and tucked into a grilled ham and cheese sandwich with a fruit smoothie. Saved.

The return journey up the track was slightly disorientating as most of it was in the pitch black. Thank goodness for the mobile phone torch. With a couple of bottles of water secured, I was ready to settle for the night, never mind the heat. But what was all this noise? My ears suddenly tuned in to the cacophony all around me – outside, hundreds of frogs croaking and cicadas chirping in the paddy field, and inside, geckos chattering on the ceiling. And I'm a light sleeper. This was going to be interesting. But this night I was so tired I could have slept through anything.

I woke up to a beautiful sunny day and enjoyed a large breakfast of fabulous fresh fruit, scrambled egg and banana pancake. Today was a free day, tomorrow was the group welcome meeting at the shala. I had read about the really cool market in town and decided to explore that in the morning. I found it without trouble and it was as I imagined it. Hustling, bustling, busy, noisy, colourful and lots to look at. Clothing, handbags, jewellery, woodwork, art, Hindu symbols and artefacts, incense. I knew I was supposed to barter but didn't have the confidence so ended up paying a ridiculous price for two very pretty cotton shawls/sheets and two sarongs. I felt proud of myself anyway. Later in the day I walked up the track in the other direction from the yoga centre to see what was there. I found a serene countryside of rice paddy fields with the odd house dotted about. Chickens and ducks roamed freely. I came upon a little café and sat looking at the pretty view while sipping from a freshly cut coconut. The café had a spa attached to it, so I spontaneously booked a massage for the following morning. Wasn't that working with "living in the present moment"? I thought so.

Back at my bungalow I joined a Facebook conversation with other course participants. People had been arriving from all over the world. We seemed to be spread out a little but everyone knew where the high street was. It was agreed we'd meet outside Starbucks at seven (see? It's not only me...) and find somewhere to have dinner. I hoped it would be fun, although apprehension about being on my own in a strange place began morphing into apprehension about fitting into the group. It was clear that the others were much younger than me, which is what I had expected. In the diary that I kept for the first five days (after which I had no time to write anything), that afternoon I wrote:

I'm over my 24-hour freak-out which is great, I just hope I can manage the course physically. The programme is hard as it is, but in this heat and humidity... I don't want to be the "old one" collapsing.

I also added, *Been thinking about Hamish and life at home – I want to get into a different groove when I get back, more togetherness. We're ever so far apart at the moment.*

The dinner did turn out to be fun, I met half the group, a diverse mix of nationalities and stages of life.

The following day was a big deal. The welcoming ceremony was in the shala where the whole group gathered and met the teaching team for the first time. A place had been laid out for each of us in a circle on the floor, decorated with beautiful flowers, and included our coursework booklets. In the middle of the circle and arranged in bright orange blossom was the word WELCOME. It was stunning. It was now that I really got a sense of the group as we had to introduce ourselves in turn. It was very young – the majority were in their twenties – and female (only two guys). There was only one other lady, called Sandra, my age, and we were the only married people. I was the only parent, nobody else had children (and that included the teachers). In a group of 25 people that felt significant somehow although I wasn't sure why. I noticed some of them were the same age that Francesca would have been if she were alive. I felt something stir just a little in my heart but quickly moved my thoughts on.

The teachers outlined the course programme but gave us the class schedule for the first week only, to prevent us from getting distracted with thinking too far ahead. It looked amazing – anatomy, philosophy, yoga *asana* practice, meditation. Included was an optional evening *bhajan* (singing devotional hymns together) which would be weekly. To fit in all this content, our only free day was Sunday. Breakfast and lunch were provided but we were responsible for our own evening meals.

To enhance our yoga experience, there would be two other things we were to participate in. Firstly, we were to practise *seva*. This means selfless service, where you do something without expectation of result or reward and is meant to be of benefit for all. Various jobs had been written on folded pieces of paper, put in a bowl and passed around the circle for us to pick one. My *seva* was to mix and refill the yoga mat cleaning sprays at the end of every week, and also to take the mat cleaning towels to be washed at the cleaners in town and collect them when ready. Jobs other people got were ringing the bell to signal return to class, taking attendance, lowering the straw blinds of the shala to shield the sun, sweeping the shala floor and so on.

The second thing we were to do was practise the *Yamas* and *Niyamas* of Patanjali. This was really exciting and confirmed I had made the right yoga school choice. I reflected back to my day with Alan Shearer and how I had struggled with applying the yogic themes to my behaviour. Well, there was no escaping now. Once again, bits of paper with a *Yama* (attitude towards others) or a *Niyama* (attitude towards yourself) written on it were put in the bowl and passed around the circle. We were to pick one and channel whatever we had chosen for the duration of the yoga course. I happened to be last and picked up the one piece of paper left. The universe had chosen for me *Satya* - the *Yama* of truthfulness, honesty and integrity. This was interesting, I thought, I would make sure to read more about this later.

There was, however, a slight adjustment to the week's schedule to take into account the Balinese Nyepi Day on Tuesday, a Hindu festival of silence that happened to fall at the start of our training course. We would have our classes on Monday, and in the evening we could go into town and watch the ritual procession. This would be a parade of colourful demonic statues called *ogoh-ogoh* made by the locals, symbolising negative elements or malevolent spirits. There would be a lot of noise made on purpose to drive these demons away. The following day we were to observe the 24-hour silence and stay in our respective accommodation. We were encouraged to not even speak to anyone, as the day is reserved for self-reflection. The religious purpose of the silence was to fool the demons into thinking there was no one residing there and they would leave the island alone. To this end, the whole island would observe the silence. The airport would be closed and all the ports. There would be no travelling or milling about whatsoever, the restaurants and shops would be closed, and no lighting of fires. The only people allowed out would be the *Pecalang*, the traditional security men who patrolled the streets to ensure the rules were being followed. Fortunately for me, there would be meals provided where I was staying but everyone else had to buy food the day before. Wow, a lot going on, I tried to take it all in.

Then, with the briefing finished, we were told we were going into town for a blessing ceremony by a local priest and we needed to dress appropriately. What luck that I'd bought those pretty sheets and could wrap one of them around my waist to look like a traditional skirt. At least it was religiously respectful. Gathered once again, the group made its way down the track and to a temple just off the high street. It was a beautiful ceremony of making offerings, expressing gratitude and setting intentions. For a non-religious person like me, the whole thing had an ethereal, surreal feel. I was hanging way, way out there and it was only Day 2. Perhaps this journey would be more than just yoga teacher training?

I loved Nyepi Day. I woke up to complete silence, wildlife excluded of course. No planes, no revving mopeds, no jarring car horns, no construction or machinery noise. This is what the world sounded like before industry, motor engines and electricity – how fabulous! Imagine, a whole day to yourself, not required to speak or be anywhere at any time, nor to do anything. All we had been asked to consider by the teachers were two beautiful yoga asana practices, one for the morning and one for the afternoon. I decided to do those and to refresh myself about the *Yamas* and *Niyamas*, especially *Satya*. Eating breakfast in silence with the other students also living at the hostel felt very peaceful. I felt relieved to not have pressure to engage in conversation, to decide whether to sit with someone or not.

This was particularly welcome as I had struggled slightly the evening before when the full group had gone to see the parade. It was reminiscent of the first day of school, an experience I think I overdosed on as a young person, attending as I did seven educational institutions in three different countries between 4 and 19 years old. Since leaving Norway age 10, wherever I was, I was "foreign". I had an accent. Would I be accepted now? It had certainly been a rough ride in the two experiential groups during my counselling training (at the beginning of the counselling diploma course I was once referred to as "the outsider"), and maybe I was still sensitive from that. I had time to reflect in my diary on Nyepi Day:

[last night at the parade] I noticed my constant concern about who was talking to whom, and whether was I being included. At one point I very nearly left altogether to eat dinner alone and go home. I was very tired, but it was more than that. It was wanting to escape the feeling of not being part of the group. I resisted this temptation, however, and ended up having a lovely dinner with some young women who were fun, no sense of rejection at all. I am the source and creator of my

own insecurity. Had I left, I would have missed the laughter, the helpful advice and information about local activities and the training course. I would have missed hearing others' stories, doubts and similar concerns about what's ahead. By not letting my fear get the better of me, I gained so much more. I can see that being aloof is off-putting to others and leads to the very thing you are trying to avoid: isolation.

For the first time, I think ever, I had a real sense of contentment. Not happiness, but *contentment*. The two are not the same. You are content when you are satisfied with what there is, just as it is. What you have is sufficient, you don't need more. Happiness is often sought "out there", it's a response to a trigger. For example, we think of it in terms of someone or something making us happy. Contentment comes completely from within. It's not chasing that feel-good high, it's simply gratitude for what you've got already. I understood this now. With a day of not worrying about who was doing what, when and with whom, I could soften a little. I wanted to try and lean into the group and relax into the experience.

I enjoyed reading about *Satya* in the training material. Truthfulness is more than not lying. It's about accepting the world as it is and understanding that reality is a selective act of attention and interpretation. This means "truth" is different to different people. When your thoughts agree with your words, and your words agree with your actions, you are practising integrity. There is a tendency to talk, to communicate too much. We try to convince others of our relative truths, which unsurprisingly leads to competitive arguments. Intolerance gives rise to a habit of using subtle forms of verbal violence in the name of "your personal truth". There was a quote in the training manual that leapt out:

Most people do not listen with the intent to understand; they listen with the intent to reply. (S R Covey).

But I knew this already, right? I mean, I was a trained counsellor, I'm trained to listen. I spent five years working with people's truths. And yet I'd been given *Satya* as the *Yama* to channel for the month. Maybe I needed to look at things closer to home then. Did I act with integrity there, in my marriage? Well, I felt very frustrated because *I* was the one not being heard. That was my *samskara*.

Although I had read about Patanjali's Eight Limbs of Yoga before, it was different contemplating it on a balcony in a Bali jungle on Nyepi Day, with instructions to put it into practice. I needed to take a closer look. Reading the *Yamas* in order, I realised that the first of the five *Yamas*, *Ahimsa*, meaning non-violence, was closely linked to the second, *Satya*. So, not hitting or killing someone is obvious enough. But what about the more subtle mind stuff? For example, generating your own negativity and projecting it into others is a form of violence. So is verbally putting people down. Talking badly about someone behind their back. Undermining or belittling someone. Envy. Deliberately setting people up against each other. Mind games such as trying to make someone feel jealous. All forms of prejudice – religious, racist, sexist etc. And so on. These things can be done without even raising one's voice or laying a finger on the person, but the *intention* is harmful. War and any form of physical abuse and violence are clear. But damaging the environment is also violence, from over-fishing and burning down the Amazon rain forest to littering or fly-tipping.

So, if you apply the concept more broadly, you quickly realise how far-reaching *Ahimsa* is. No wonder *Ahimsa* is on top of the list of how to conduct yourself towards others. What about me then? Thinking about it honestly, I had been practicing some subtle verbal "violence" at times towards Hamish. I communicated frustration by pointing out what he was not doing, not saying, not giving. By radiating dissatisfaction. Coming at the relationship from a perspective of who was right and who was wrong, with me being right. This really was the truth.

In my diary I wrote a *"Memo to self"*, a list of behaviours outlined in the reading that are harmful to ourselves and to others and solve absolutely nothing:

Negative facial expressions
Anger
Accusations
Manipulation
Provocation
Judgement

Grudges
Bitterness
Frustration
Resentment
Complaining
Projection

I had to admit I'd had a go with these in the marriage and not got a lot to show for it. Other than feeling drained and exhausted. I'm sure the recipient felt the same. Okay, so more *Satya* and *Ahimsa* required going forward then.

The first week progressed on different levels. Intellectually, the course offered more than I could have hoped for. So thorough, so much information, the challenge was to take it all in. I looked forward to every class. Physically, I found the climate harder to manage than I had expected. I was surprised because I had coped all right with the African heat several times by this time. But that was the relatively dry Equatorial sun. I was in the jungle now. With 90% + humidity levels I was never not sweating, day and night. I started to feel nauseous and developed a runny tummy. Fortunately, I realised that this was not the food but the dehydration. Yes, I was drinking copious amounts of water, but my electrolyte/salt balance was completely off. I was glad that I had brought electrolyte sachets with me, and as soon as I added the powder to my drinking water I felt fine.

And then the rain, oh my god! Although the monsoon season was meant to be over, we had a spell of it in that first week. I had not experienced such weather. It felt like being pounded by golf ball sized water bombs. Continuous sheets of drenching wetness for hours and days on end. It made the English "cloudburst" feel very tame in comparison. You know the film *Singing in the Rain* with Gene Kelly? When I first saw that film, I laughed at the scene where he's dancing down that street in torrents because I didn't think it was very realistic. I dubbed it "Hollywood rain". Well, I can tell you that in the jungle it rains just like that. And as the water drops pounded the earth so hard, it splashed mud and dirt up the legs. It was impossible to keep clean. My feet kept sliding in my permanently squidgy and slimy flip-flops. I found myself running like mad between shelters trying to dodge it which was utterly futile. I never knew that rain could feel so, well, *hostile. Everything* was wet. Between the humidity and the rain, the level of moisture in the air meant that nothing would dry. So you would shower and use a towel that was still damp from the previous shower. I stopped washing my clothes because yeah, there was nowhere I could hang them to dry. I heard some other students laughing over how they had found mould in their wardrobes, growing on the rucksacks and clothes that they weren't using…

Sleep was also a challenge. You'd think the 12-hour yoga days would be enough to knock me out, but the heat combined with all the reptile/amphibian nocturnal din would get the better of me. The curse of being a light sleeper… I really didn't want this to get in the way though.

Socially, I gradually got to know the others, especially the students who were also staying in the same accommodation. The lady from Tasmania called Sandra was one of them, and she and I would joke about being the "older ones". We became good friends, shopping at the market and eating out together. I couldn't have got through the training without her. But the youthfulness of the group was also significant for me. It had an intense, vibrant energy that began to seep into my skin and into my consciousness. An awakening. In all my pain and trying to survive for the last 25 years since I was their age, I had long forgotten what it felt like to be like them, like my younger self. Collectively they packed a powerful punch of positivity, confidence and fearlessness. Listening to them discussing their plans for the future, it was clear they felt there was nothing they couldn't do. They were so unrestrained and free in their thought and expectations. The world really was their oyster. Such belief. Such empowerment! Not to mention their beauty. I could see the beauty in everyone.

I had arrived with the aim to immerse myself in yoga only. My intention had been to not talk about Francesca because I didn't need to. But with the harsh environment, the tiredness and the supportive vibe of the group, it was futile to resist. My cracks started to appear. In the first week we were all offered a one-to-one meeting with one of the two lead teachers as an opportunity to check in and share whatever we needed to share. I rocked up to my appointment with Burkhard all mature and controlled, sat down and when asked how I was doing I promptly began to talk about Francesca and cry. I literally had no control at all, it came out of its own accord. I felt a bit silly, but even this was washed away by the tears. I didn't care. There was no judgement, only understanding and empathy.

I tentatively shared my loss with a few of the young people (and Sandra, of course, who was awesome) and, instead of the shock and revulsion that I was expecting (which had happened to me before), came only acceptance, support and what felt like love. I understood why the universe had chosen this group for me – they were healers. They could see, acknowledge and contain my pain. I think that being the only parent in the group made it safe to open up, knowing from experience how uncomfortable it is for people with children to hear about child death because it's scary and disturbing obviously. I felt my grip loosen around my heart a little bit more.

And it wasn't only me. Over the course of the month I think most people cried at some point, we all had our stuff. Youth is no barrier to carrying a burden. I knew this from my own experience and from counselling young people. The collective healing force touched everyone, helped liberate and lighten everyone. At least I sincerely hope it did.

But there was more to come. As I came to the end of the second week with the halfway point in my sights, I realised I would need to change accommodation to something more manageable. Maybe it would have been okay if I were on holiday and able to have a relaxed agenda, but I needed to be mentally and physically strong for the long study days. The heat, humidity and poor sleep were getting to me. I needed to be surrounded by proper walls. I would FaceTime Hamish every now and then, and just the sight of him wearing a cosy cashmere jumper would make me cry. He wasn't sweating profusely. He looked so *comfortable*!

I looked online and found a nice hotel with air-conditioned rooms and a pool not far from the yoga centre. It was walkable to and from town as well as the yoga centre. Perfect. I checked availability and heaved a sigh of relief as they had a room for the last week of the course. I booked it, thinking I could pull out one more week where I was. My main concern was being discreet and not making a fuss. I felt embarrassed to "bow out" in this way, but needs must, I had to look after myself. I felt lifted just knowing I had a moving out date.

I went to bed on the Thursday night that second week hoping for a half decent sleep. I was very tired and fell asleep quickly. I suddenly woke up with a start, confused and wondering what was happening. I felt burning, painful hot pricking on my abdomen, upper thighs and literally between my legs. Yeah, that's right... there. In the dark I couldn't see anything, so I fumbled for my mobile phone on the floor and turned on its light. Now I could see the long trail of teeny tiny ants that were coming up and over the edge of the mattress by my head, underneath the mosquito net, from below the bed somewhere. The line came around my body and dispersed around my middle where they were biting me. Well, I was fully awake now! I thrashed about trying to kill as many as I could, but how to stop more from coming? The net was clearly useless for these guys. I got out of bed and found my roll-on insecticide. I then got back in and rolled the liquid along the sheet in a circle around me, kind of like a circle of wagons forming a protective barrier against external attack. The idea was the ants would not want to cross the line.

By the time I had done all this I really was fully awake. Please let it be no earlier than 5.30 am, or even 5.00 am. I could manage that. I looked at my mobile phone. It was 1.30 am. I just lay there, unable to fall back to sleep, letting the tears of anger, frustration and sheer exhaustion come. I had gone over the sleep deprivation edge. I needed to move as soon as possible. So, in the middle of that night I went online again and said a prayer as I checked whether I could get that room for two weeks instead. It looked like I could, but I'd need to get it confirmed by the hotel in the morning.

Eventually the next day dawned. I wasn't sure whether I could manage that morning's pre-breakfast yoga practice but turned up anyway. To my joy it was announced that the practice would be yin yoga, the less exertive but deeper yoga style. Yes, this would be okay, no one need know what state I was in. I think it was near the end of that practice but I can't remember exactly, or which yoga posture I was in (it might have been Reclining Bound Angle pose, *Supta Baddha Konasana*, lying in a strong backbend position on top of a bolster), but suddenly I just cracked. I rolled over onto one side into a foetal position and started to cry. Quietly but uncontrollably. Wave after wave of grief

142

washed over me, I lost sense of time and space. I was the grief, I was the pain. And all I could hear in my ears, which I mouthed silently over and over again was "not for the last time", "not for the last time". I could hear Francesca's voice repeating it. And then I finally got it, ten years later, what was behind her words. We weren't parting for the last time because we are always together. Our essence was the same and we were joined forever through it. It's just that she made the return to Source and I was still here. In this moment I didn't just understand it intellectually but really *felt* it and *knew* it.

The class finished and people filed out for breakfast, respectfully leaving me there. I couldn't move. Eventually one of the teachers came back to the shala and sat with me for a while, hugging me and encouraging me to let the grief go – she knew of my loss. I managed to have some breakfast but skipped the next class. I had to be on my own for a bit. The hotel confirmed the room availability and I agreed check-in for the following morning.

As I relaxed into my new "home" I wasn't angry about the bungalow and my experience there at all. I could absolutely see that it would take flying to the other side of the world, living in a jungle with kind-hearted strangers, sleep deprivation and a long line of tiny biting ants to help me let go and soften. Brutal though it was, I needed that figurative crowbar to open up my heart. Why? And why did the universe conspire to have it happen at that moment in the training? Because teaching is not just giving instructions, is it? You're giving a part of yourself too, you put your heart into the offering. Hence the expression "put your heart and soul into [something]", right? If your heart is closed, your offering won't be complete, won't be *authentic*. You couldn't channel *Satya*. People would sense it in my energy. No, what happened absolutely needed to happen. And let's not forget the yogic philosophy: the path to enlightenment is through pain and suffering. Oh yes, it is indeed.

The rest of the course flew by. On the Saturday morning I was moving rooms, we had been given the programme for the third week and the schedule for teaching our first class. I was terrified. I think we were all terrified. And when I looked at the timings, I was first up on that Monday! I only had Sunday to prepare, so no time to take a whole day off. But I managed it and felt very proud afterwards. It was the first time I had ever formally taught, and even though it was scary, of course, it also felt natural to me. It felt *right*. Something had shifted.

It was good to get that out of the way as I could relax the rest of the week. I set up a new routine. I spoke to the hotel and booked a scooter taxi to take me to the yoga centre every morning at 6.30 am to get to the first class. It was the same lovely young man each day, and it was fabulous to start the day with this ride, watching the sun rise over the rice paddy fields as we sped down the bumpy track. I had found a beautiful statue of Ganesha in the hotel garden. Ganesha is the Hindu God represented by an elephant and is the remover of all obstacles.

Well, that felt appropriate to me, I needed all the help I could get. I made sure to pass this statue every day and pause there to say a little prayer on my way to the morning scooter lift. Then, depending on what was going on, I'd walk back after the last class and have dinner on my own, or after eating out with friends. Naughty trips to the market and jewellery shops with Sandra happened during lunch breaks and the last weekend. I enjoyed those times so much, we had great fun. We bartered as a team, our prize acquisition and best deal being a statuette of the Dancing Shiva each. Thank you so much, dear Sandra. By the end of the course, I had acquired some beautiful things to keep and to give as gifts at home.

During the last week we had to teach a full-length class, and although I was nervous, I wasn't as tense this time. The instruction we had been given, especially the workshop on how to adjust people safely, made me feel well prepared. And we supported each other through it. We were split into groups, taking turns teaching to our group, and I was amazed at how different each of us were. It was beautiful to watch the different presentations, the individual ways of offering the teaching. To receive the yoga direct from their heart and soul. A piece of themselves, that's what it felt like. I hope that's what I felt like to them.

Graduation Day arrived and we were all so excited. The joy, relief and pride were palpable in the air, in the shala, everywhere. We were not the same people who had arrived four weeks earlier. We had all shifted some stuff. I certainly had. We ended as we had started, in a big circle on the deck of the shala. Once again, seating places were laid for us decorated with beautiful flowers. In the centre of the circle, spelled out in bright orange flowers, were the words *INTO THE* and a big heart shaped and filled with red flowers. Yes indeed, *into the heart*. That had been my Bali journey destination in the end.

Each student was called up to receive their diploma, a gift (a book full of yogic quotes, sayings and poems compiled by the teachers) and a flower lei necklace. We honoured each other with a good cheer and clapping each time. When my name was called and I found myself walking up to the teachers it was like an out of body experience. Floaty and surreal. I hugged each teacher, thanking them, but no words could really express the profound gratitude I felt. And when I turned to face the group, a huge cheer ringing in my ears, I couldn't say anything at all. I just shed a few tears of joy.

I was ready to go home now. I felt a strong pull to return and begin again. A month of reflecting on *Satya* made me determined to inject more energy into my marriage, to make it work. To find a connection. That was my thought as I watched Ubud high street recede through the back window of the taxi on my way back to the airport. And as the plane accelerated down the runway I felt my spirits lift as we became airborne. Taking in the last glimpse of jungle from the air, it looked so beautiful, so benign! I left a lot of stuff behind me there for sure, my load lighter than when I arrived.

"When are you going to start teaching? I'm desperate to get back into my yoga."

I hadn't been back long when Sarah asked the question. I was still assimilating everything I had learned and not sure about what yoga direction to take, if any. But Sarah's enthusiasm was unrelenting as well as infectious, so I agreed to teach her privately. Soon after, another friend of hers wanted to try yoga, so I did one-to-one sessions with her. I spent a happy summer with these two lovely ladies putting my instruction into practice and developing my own offering. It felt *right*.

As August drew to a close, and with Sarah's support, I felt confident enough to set up a group class. I needed to find the right space and eventually found a lovely village hall just minutes from my house that was available to rent. A peaceful location away from the hustle and bustle of town and nestled beneath the Downs, the ridge of hills now officially an area of outstanding natural beauty and that had Francesca's spirit all over it.

I'm happy to say that yoga turned out to be my spiritual home, a place of peace, calm and security. It's where I work on my body and spiritual awareness. It's where I work out the issues. And if you had told me this as I walked down those steps on the last day at the London corporate headquarters eleven years before, I would have laughed in your face. But I can see how the universe had laid a trail for me. Everyone I met played their part in guiding me forward. The executives, the counselling clients, the yoga students.

From the office, to the therapy room, to the mat.

Seek refuge in the attitude of detachment and you
will amass wealth of spiritual awareness.
Bhagavad Gita 2.49

Chapter 8: A is for Asperger's

If I ask myself honestly, had I always known there was something going on in the background, something unusual? Looking back with 20/20 hindsight the answer is yes of course, my instinctive alarm bells had gone off on occasion but the moments always passed. Life was busy, there was no time to pause when the bells rang. I just parked these incidents in the back of my mind somewhere.

This part of my story spans the whole of "after Francesca". In fact, it began before. I met Hamish at work, although we were based in completely different parts of the same company. I was in London and he was in Sweden. Occasionally our paths crossed at head office and at business events. Hamish was a senior figure, well respected and popular with his team. He was an excellent speaker and presenter. I was attracted to his charm and sense of humour, you were never far away from a witty remark or a joke. A cardiologist by background, he had a strong creative side as well.

He introduced me to his hobby, and obvious talent, of landscape photography right at the beginning, bringing photos to show me at our first dinner together.

It wasn't love at first sight by any means, more a slow convergence. When I wasn't working in London I was at my rental house near the family home looking after the girls. Malcolm and I managed Francesca's health issues all the while, which sometimes involved spells in hospital. With his medical knowledge, Hamish proved to be very helpful in this regard. Having him to discuss treatment options and the latest health crisis with soothed the family's nerves. So, with the raw emotions of the divorce year behind us, a new, albeit unusual, family unit emerged. Rather than the predictable splitting that comes with divorce, which would have been Malcolm on one side and Hamish and I on the other, with the girls in between, what actually happened was Hamish joining the family of four to make it five.

I think this is when I first felt that perhaps something was different. I would be away on a business trip to discover Hamish had been invited around to dinner at Malcolm's. It was very adult of Malcolm to include him in this way, but equally big of Hamish to accept. Ex-husbands and new partners don't often befriend each other. No matter, because the girls loved it, Francesca especially. She enjoyed teasing Hamish at dinner by insisting on him having seconds of something naughty and then telling on him. So, I'd be sitting in some hotel room in Frankfurt getting ready for the next day of business meetings and receive a text from Francesca saying "Hamish just ate a second Yorkshire pudding!" It became a family joke and Hamish was not bothered in the least. We all got along and Hamish remained his dynamic, funny, doctor self. He was generous and kind. We were good together.

After two years, the opportunity to consolidate houses and take the next step came up. I left my rental and Hamish sold his house up north so we could buy a house together locally to be close to the family home. Four months later Francesca died.

If alarm bells had gone off and I had ignored them before, I could not ignore them now. Hamish's reaction to Francesca's death was off the wall. No tears, no emotion. He said the right words like "that's sad" and "what a shame" but there was no apparent feeling in them. Being overwhelmed with shock and grief, I was unable to process it at all. Two weeks after the funeral he announced we really needed to "get back to business", meaning get back to whatever he thought normal was, and left me to sort out the broken dishwasher when he went to work. He attended all his office Christmas festivities without hesitation. I did not attend mine.

What the hell was going on? I felt doubtful about our relationship but unclear in what way. The absence of emotion and understanding was a huge contrast to how I had known him, and it was deeply upsetting. It made no sense. Unsure of what it meant and what to do, I did nothing. Malcolm, Karina and I were neck deep in our own grief. Any more drama or break-up would have been intolerable, especially for Karina who had gone through a parental divorce, a house move and the loss of her sister within three years. So I let it go.

A year later I decided to leave the company, as you know, and Hamish was instrumental in helping me forge a new career. He was financially supportive and keen for me to find work I really enjoyed doing. But had I tuned into a pattern? Was there something about inappropriate responses to my and others' emotional cues and needs? He didn't seem to register another person's upset or distress. And yet a lot of things did work between us. We had fun travelling and enjoyed cultural interests like the theatre and art exhibitions. So when we got married four years after Francesca died I thought that on balance we were good to go.

Then there followed a slow but perceptible shift over time. The dynamic, funny doctor was replaced with a depressed, anxious, negative character I didn't recognise, and a new status quo took shape – when I was fine, everything was fine, but when I was not fine, it fell apart. Any expressed upset coming from me was met with anger and agitation or a complete blank and withdrawal. But here was the confusing part – he continued to be the charming doctor to everyone else. When we were with other people – work do's, family gatherings, socialising at home or out – he seemed his familiar self. It just didn't make any sense. To his credit, when I suggested marriage counselling he agreed. But after a few sessions I could see we weren't getting anywhere. In the counselling room he was the doctor, displaying behaviour totally absent at home like listening attentively and choosing his answers carefully. Being the perfect counselling client, in other words.

Life went on. I swung between ignoring the issue completely and trying to find a solution. If I could just figure it out, find the answer, then everything would be alright. I was a counsellor after all. Was it to do with him going to boarding school? I researched it and found a book called *The Psychological Trauma of the 'Privileged' Child* by Dr Joy Schaverien. Yes, Boarding School Syndrome is an actual thing. Hamish had been sent away for five years, aged 13 to 18, to a private boys' school, ironically within a local bus ride from his home. Some aspects of this syndrome did fit: it "can cause major problems in adulthood: depression, an inability to talk about or understand emotions, the urge to escape from or destroy intimate relationships". Other attitudes that resonated were "self-reliance, high moral values, pride in endurance, acute discomfort in asking for help, denial of pain and overachiever but may underestimate self". The only thing that didn't quite fit was Hamish being relatively old when he left home at 13. This syndrome is mostly linked to people who were sent away at a much younger age, such as seven or eight. But still...

I talked to Hamish about it and he actually did a little reading on the subject. He acknowledged the relevance but that was it. And this was the most frustrating part. No matter how I came at the problem – with a book, an idea or just an angry meltdown – nothing ever changed. I simply couldn't get any traction. He got up every day and got on with what he wanted to do as if the previous day and what had been said never happened. I likened it to the Bill Murray film *Groundhog Day*. That was what my marriage felt like. Inside my head I was going around in circles tormenting myself. What had I missed? It hadn't been like this before so why did it change? What had I done? Anger and resentment were never far from the surface, especially in social settings where he made an effort for other people. It was impossible to not walk my *samskara* of "it's not about me". I felt increasingly lonely and low. I was losing touch with my usual fun-loving upbeat self. I repeatedly would say I just felt like the housekeeper, like paid staff, but got no response.

So here is where I distracted myself with the dog, friends and yoga. After Bali I had hoped to find a way forward. The marriage had not turned out as I had expected but the rest of my life was decent. Hamish was a good provider, I lacked for nothing, he supported any pursuits I felt would be helpful to me. He just had this really tricky flipside – when emotion was required it wasn't there. He never asked me what I was thinking or feeling about anything. He remained kind and generous, just disengaged. And he continued his quirky habit of not being able to enter the room without making a negative statement, normally related to the BBC News.

By now I had met Sarah and shared my story with

her. One morning we were out on a dog walk together.

"Have you considered that he may have Asperger's?" she said after I had shared yet another tale of frustration.

"What? Asperger's?" I was taken aback by her suggestion. "You mean autistic?"

"Yes." It wasn't without thought she'd offered it. A close family member had autism so she knew what she was talking about.

"No, that can't be," I dismissed, "he is socially totally adept, which autistic people aren't. Whenever we are with other people he's fine." I remembered the autistic counselling clients I had worked with. No, I definitely would have picked something like that up at the beginning.

We left it there.

Another year passed with more yoga, Barley and friends to fill the emotional gap in my life. We were essentially living separate lives by this time – me at home and he in London during the week, with weekends spent catching up on house chores. We only felt together when we travelled, like to Uganda. Then in summer 2018 a family discussion led to a particularly inappropriate and over the top reaction from Hamish that I just couldn't ignore. It tipped me over the edge and I was seething with rage. I had had enough. There was something very wrong with him and I had to find out what. It was imperative I understand it because if I was going to leave the marriage I at least needed to know why.

To date, something had kept holding me back. What was it?

It didn't take me long on Google to find it. Maybe I had Sarah's remarks still ringing in my ears, but there it was as plain as day: Asperger's. Before I get all technical, let me just say that the autistic spectrum is like the female menopause – no two people are exactly the same, the manifestation is unique to each individual. There are some aspects, however, that are common but vary in degree of presentation. Named after the Austrian paediatrician Johann Friedrich Karl Asperger (1906-1980) who identified it, Asperger's is a neurological disorder in the brain which affects, among other things, the ability to read and express emotions. The National Autistic Society states that "autism is more common than most people think. There are around 700,000 autistic people in the UK, including those with Asperger's. That's more than 1 in 100."

So what is it exactly? The diagnostic criteria for Asperger's Disorder according to the DSM – IV (American Psychiatric Association 2000) includes social impairments such as:

- *The lack of social and emotional reciprocity*
- *Difficulties in understanding social situations and other people's thoughts and feelings*
- *Tendency to think of issues as being black-and-white rather than considering multiple perspectives in a flexible way*

- *Frequent tendency to say things without considering the emotional impact on the listener*
- *A lack of spontaneous interest in sharing experiences with others*

Asperger's also includes restricted, repetitive, and stereotyped patterns of behaviour, interests and activities, such as:

- *Preoccupation with one or more stereotyped and restricted pattern of interest*
- *Inflexible adherence to specific routines or rituals*
- *Stereotyped repetitive motor mannerisms*

(Source: www.theneurotypical.com and Tony Attwood, *The Complete Guide to Asperger's Syndrome*)

There was a bit more information that caught my attention:

The person with Asperger's is unaware of what their loved ones think or feel, and even when told, he can only see things from his point of view. With limited empathy for others, connecting with a loved one is extremely difficult, so those with Asperger's Syndrome go through life focused on their own needs and wants and often miss what is going on with others.

(Source: www.theneurotypical.com)

I recognised Hamish here but perhaps not so extreme. A more toned-down version. He lacked strict rituals and motor mannerisms, for example, both of which I would have noticed straight away. Reading on through the literature I also recognised myself, now defined as the "neurotypical partner":

People involved with a [AS] partner report feeling invalidated, unsupported, unheard, unknown and uncared-for." This can result in *"depression, loneliness, anger, low self-esteem, emotional breakdown…*
(Source: www.theneurotypical.com)

Tony Attwood is the go-to expert on AS, and in his book *The Complete Guide to Asperger's Syndrome* his description of the neurotypical partner really hit home for me:

- *Men with AS seek partners who compensate for their difficulties, who are at the other end of social and emotional abilities, i.e. very maternal.* (So I'm thinking a counsellor would fit the brief perfectly).
- *The most common problem for [neurotypicals] is feeling lonely… although the couple are living together, conversations may be few, and primarily involve the exchange of information rather than an enjoyment of each other's company, experiences and shared opinions.*
- *Neurotypical partners complain 'it is never his fault', 'I always get the blame'… and they feel emotionally exhausted and neglected.*

- *During times of personal distress, when empathy and words and gestures of affection would be expected as an emotional restorative, the neorotypical partner may be left to 'get over it'.*

Wow. Well, there it all was. My mind reeled from one bizarre episode to another in the past, every scenario now fully explained. Hamish's response to Francesca's death, the absence of his own friends, the absence of meaningful family relationships, the blame game, the blanking, the lack of connection, the depression, the negativity, the anxiety and so on. At first I felt relieved. So, it wasn't me. I wasn't going crazy. No wonder my approaches of "if I could just change myself this will work" and "if I could just change him this will work" were going nowhere! The relief was in discovering it really wasn't a case of *won't* but *can't*. When you stop to think about it, there is a huge difference between the two.

Reading further in Attwood's book, my eye caught a killer statement:

The relationship is just fine for their AS needs, while their partner feels more like a housekeeper, accountant and mother figure.

Oh my god, had I read that right? Yes, it actually said *housekeeper*. It seemed I was nothing but a neurotypical cliché! My relief quickly gave way to anger. How the hell had I missed all this? How had

158

I not seen the whole picture fully at the beginning?
The answer was there in black-and-white:

[The neurotypical partners] never saw the real person before they were married. And after their wedding day, the person abandoned the persona that was previously so attractive.

And how do they manage to create this persona, this façade of normalcy?

Initially a woman may admire the man's intelligence, knowledge, good manners, old-fashioned sensibilities, unconventional charm, childlike qualities and his practical, rational way of looking at the world. He may have a good job…

Yes, tick to all that.

Although the deficits of a man with Asperger's become painfully clear in time, they often present as normal in the beginning of a relationship… Many study the words and behaviour of neurotypical people around them and copy it. They learn exactly what they should do and say in a romantic relationship since none of it comes naturally to them.

So was I duped? This felt really uncomfortable, I have to say. I knew instinctively that it was true, that Hamish had Asperger's, but a conscious misrepresentation of himself to ensnare me in some way, was he capable of that? What about all the acts of kindness and support? His friendship with Malcolm? I now understood how that worked, though – Hamish would not pick up on the social awkwardness of it because he couldn't apply an emotional filter like judgement. So it wouldn't occur to him to not be friends just because he was my ex-husband. And our family unit had benefited hugely from this, the girls especially. I remained bereft of answers and felt I needed help, because what was I to do now with this awareness, this knowledge?

Back to Google I went, where I found a neurotypical support group called *Different Together*. Reading about the various testimonials of NT partners it became very clear, and it's worth repeating, that every Asperger's person and every AS-NT partnership described was unique. No two experiences were the same. There were couples who had managed to make adjustments and stay together, while other neurotypicals were clearly angry and in the middle of divorce proceedings. If I was looking for a recipe to follow I wasn't going to find it here, or indeed anywhere. However, the group made me feel acknowledged and less alone which was very helpful. I felt *heard*. I wasn't the only one facing this situation and that calmed my nerves.

My dilemma now was whether to tell Hamish or not. I threw the question out into the group and got a mixed response. Some said their AS partner had reacted badly and dismissed it completely, while others said it was a moment of positive turning point and huge relief to the AS person. I remember one lady said that either way, the AS person was not going to change fundamentally. So, I could see it was more a case of adaptation, not transformation. Whichever direction my marriage was going to go, it would be my call.

I didn't know what to do so I did nothing. I decided to wait and just sit with it. It wasn't easy. My *samskara* of the abandoned child kept drawing me into self-pity, into the victim: I wasn't married to the person I thought I'd married, I didn't have the relationship I wanted. I suffered from couple envy looking at people around me, especially those displaying affection for each other. I was chased by thoughts like "hadn't I been through enough?", "hadn't I suffered enough?", "after all my loss now this as well?" And so on.

Then in October that same year, we went to Edinburgh for the weekend. Hamish wanted to do some family history research there. We were in a café when he suddenly got all agitated about what I was saying about my yoga business, something about the fee that I was charging was wrong. He wouldn't stop going on and on, not listening to me, and suddenly I thought "right, this is it, I'm going to tell him." I couldn't stand it any longer, I'd roll the dice and take the consequences.

I raised my hand with palm facing him and said, "Hamish, please stop for a second and just listen to yourself. You're all agitated and you're upsetting me. I've got something important to tell you and I'm just going to say it."

He paused and went silent.

"I think you've got Asperger's. You're on the autistic spectrum."

He said nothing for a long moment, then, "well, that would explain a lot."

Oh good! We were going to be able to talk about it at least. And we did, over that cup of coffee. I went through all the things that it did explain about him, about us, and he was accepting. I could see from his demeanour he had not been disingenuous with me and deliberately hidden his autism. He may have taught himself romantic behaviour to cope with the opposite sex but not with malicious intent. He had therefore not consciously "dropped the act" after we got married. His doctor persona had helped him function in the world and successfully so. It's just that – and this was the hard thing for me and no one else – he only displayed his Asperger's inside the communal space of our house when we were alone. In all other spaces and places, in his home office and in other people's company, it remained unmanifested and undetected.

We agreed to go to Waterstones on Princes Street and get some books we could read. Later on, when we returned to our accommodation, we found the Autism Spectrum Quotient (AQ) questionnaire at the back of one of them and decided to do the test separately and compare scores. This was revealing yet unsurprising. A score of 32 to 50 was defined as "very high" with most AS people scoring around 35. Hamish scored 32. The average score for a neurotypical woman is 15. I scored 9, a "low". But what was significant wasn't just the gap in the scores, it was how we had answered the questions.

We differed hugely on how we responded to the *emotional* prompts – me very high, him very low.

I felt validated and hopeful. In true AS fashion, now that he had a numerical value, a data point, Hamish accepted the conclusion. He seemed open, so maybe we could work things out. Maybe we could be one of the couples on *Different Together* forging a fulfilling life.

Was this the turning point? Could Asperger's be a spiritual growth opportunity of sorts? Could I let go of my (neurotypical) expectations and get out of my *samskara*?

Human nature is made of faith.
A person is what his shraddha is.
Bhagavad Gita 17.3

Chapter 9: Back to the jungle

I looked down at the print on the boarding pass in my hand.

Flight BA289
from London Heathrow to Phoenix Sky Harbor
Date 29 Nov 2019, Boarding Time 14.35

How funny, I thought. Three and a half years after the Bali trip I find myself standing alone in front of the security check at Terminal 5, about to board another long-haul flight but this time going thousands (5,721) of miles west. My travel yoga mat was safely stowed in my suitcase. Destination Puerto Vallarta, Mexico, my first time to this country. I would have to spend the night at Phoenix airport and catch the first flight to Puerto Vallarta the following morning. And, like with the Bali trip, I was ready to go, I needed the break. I needed to go far, far away.

Nothing had shifted in my relationship with Hamish since the "big reveal" in Edinburgh the year before after all. My hopes had been dashed and the lady on *Different Together* had been absolutely right – real change would be unlikely. That was Asperger's. I felt tired and drained. And angry, not to mention resentful. I had tried hard to apply the yogic approach and all the learning from my reading – detachment, letting go of my *samskara* etc., etc. – but had failed. I found the daily not-listened-to, not-being-seen thing intolerable. I just couldn't ignore it, or, as Eckhart Tolle advised, let it wash over me. My head kept banging against Hamish's "wall". And since he was clearly not going to change, I had pretty much decided I wanted to leave the marriage. I would get right on it in the new year.

One thing was certain, I didn't need to deal with the grief and loss of Francesca on this trip. I had done the work and had left that behind me. So, off to Mexico. Why there?

Through my self-educational track of reading about yoga on both the physical and spiritual level, I came upon the subject of fascia and became quite interested. Fascia is the connective tissue that surrounds our whole insides from top to toe. It's one big sheath, a kind of inner lining. Imagine a one-piece fish net that stretches and contracts in different directions but remains intact. It plays a vital role in how we move, in our range of movement, and in transmitting strength. It attracted my attention because through my yoga practice I had noticed some areas of my body struggling in

165

certain postures and wondered why, especially since my strength and flexibility had greatly improved over the years. Reading about fascia, I realised that the multiple surgeries I had had in the past, almost all in the front body where there were multiple scars from incisions, were having an impact. If it was affecting me, it would certainly be relevant to yoga students with surgical and injury histories. It would be good to be informed.

Wanting to learn more, I had signed up to a movement workshop for a weekend in the summer of the previous year run by Tom Myers, one of the leaders in the field of all things fascial. It would mean a trip to Maine, USA, and a new part of America to visit. Hamish came along with his cameras. The idea was that he would do photography while I went to class.

The group was geographically diverse – two Brits including me, and the rest from all over Canada and the US – but only one guy. We were there for different reasons but most of us were bodyworkers in some way, physiotherapy, osteopathy, acupuncture and yes, quite a few yoga teachers, unsurprisingly. However, what became apparent early on was how little I still knew about anatomy, in spite of my reading. This really was a deep dive into the detailed workings of the muscular and skeletal body and I wondered whether I had made the wrong decision, the wrong choice in coming. I felt out of my depth. It was intimidating, to be honest. And this gap of mine was amplified by one person in particular.

You became aware of Diana's presence immediately when she entered the room. She led with a big smile and confidence. No wonder, her knowledge of the body was impressive. She had been a physiotherapist for decades and ran her own clinic in Montreal. She had been on the medical team for the Canadian Summer Olympic competitors twice. She was also a yoga teacher. During the workshop, the questions were varied but mine were naturally yoga related – my interest lay in fascial movement in yoga postures. There was little time to socialise and during class I hung out with an acupuncturist from New York. During one break Diana came up to me and said that she had noticed my yoga angle and was happy to help me out with my questions. I didn't get an opportunity to take her up on that though.

I came back to England with plenty of self-imposed homework and hoping to keep in touch with the acupuncturist, but this fizzled out naturally after a few email exchanges. As I continued to teach and reflect on the Maine experience, an idea started forming in my head. Looking around at the students with their different body issues, I felt it would be useful to have more guidance on how yoga could work best for them. For example, the people with scoliosis, with hip replacements, with limbs of different lengths for whatever reason, with post-operative breast cancer. Sure, I could read up on this on the internet, and believe me I did, but what I missed was guidance for when specific problems came up in class. Who could help me out?

The answer was of course obvious. Diana. Who else could speak the language of yoga and anatomy so fluently? But how to approach her when I perhaps had come across as withdrawn? I had been here before, with Joanna. But this time I not only had that learning but I had my yoga philosophy knowledge as well. I was reminded of Eknath Easwaran who wrote that "avoiding people is to forfeit an opportunity to grow," which I now knew to be the case. Okay then, I decided to give it a go and "reach out" as they say in North America. I had Diana's email address (we had shared our contact details within the group) and nothing to lose. Worst case, she didn't reply, no big deal.

So, that October I wrote to her proposing a professional relationship between us, with her as my "yoga mentor/supervisor". I explained that this had been the way I worked when I was a counsellor, with a supervisor to review client material (mandatory practice), hence my idea of applying the same model to my yoga teaching. I would prepare student case studies for us to discuss via video and pay her a fee for her time. What did she think? I hit "send", throwing it out into the universe with no attachment to results but feeling hopeful.

Diana's reply came back pretty swiftly. Yes, she remembered me. No, she had not come across this yoga supervisor idea before but yes, she was up for it, why not? I was so pleased. Pleased about the positive response to the offer but more pleased that I had overcome my initial hesitancy and subsequent fear of rejection and trusted my instinct. Taken the risk and had faith. And now I had been duly rewarded. We began pretty much straight away, I had a couple of student body issues to discuss.

It turned out to be the beginning of a mutually beneficial professional partnership but also a lovely friendship. Behind the perhaps bold exterior there was a funny, generous and loving woman. Diana's heart was as big as her intellect and I benefited from both. My yoga anatomy knowledge increased in line with my confidence, I could feel it in my teaching. I was really "getting it". Over time we shared each other's stories and unsurprisingly found plenty of overlap there. We were both familiar with the classic life defence of protecting one's soft vulnerable interior with a protective outer shell.

At one point she mentioned that she was running a yoga retreat in November and there were still places. Would I like to come? It wasn't a hard sell, to be honest, a week with Diana in an eco-resort on the western coast of Mexico. But the timing was wrong, I couldn't make it at such short notice. However, when she told me in the new year she was running the same retreat again the following November and in the same place, I was all in. I was the first to sign up and pay my deposit.

Meanwhile back at London Heathrow…. I felt the usual mix of excitement and fear of solo travel, I now had to watch my own back. I think this was one thing I liked about being on my own, about hanging myself out there in the world – I felt alive. Awake. Alert. It wasn't as scary as Bali, though, I was meeting someone I knew at the other end. Diana's organisational skills were second to none and I felt totally prepared about the travel side of things, everything had been planned meticulously. I had decided to fly out three days before the group were due to meet so I could acclimatise and sleep off the jet lag. Diana was arriving early as well so we could hang out together. With me as the only European, the rest of the group consisted of French-Canadian women and two husbands. I was the only one attending on my own but I was quite relaxed about this. I felt comfortable being independent and having the choice to dip in and out of the group. I could choose how much I wanted to share about myself. I was certainly not planning on discussing Francesca.

There is always a difference between planning a trip and then actually doing it. On paper it looked reasonable – fly to Phoenix, spend the night at an airport hotel, fly to Puerto Vallarta the next morning. Easy peasy. But then you get on the plane and as it lifts off, you do the maths as you change the time on your watch and realise just how *long* the trip is, and just how *far* you're going. Twenty-four hours in travel mode door to door. And you forget how it feels to disembark in an unfamiliar airport at night, tired, and having to figure out where to catch the hotel shuttle. And sorting out how to feed yourself. And that natural terror of the alarm not working in the morning and missing the flight. And so on.

So I was quite relieved when the plane banked to align itself for the final approach into Puerto Vallarta International Airport. But what was this? We seemed to be flying through a deep gully in a jungle with steep lush green hillsides on either side. It looked amazing, so completely foreign. I couldn't wait to get out there. Fortunately, I had had the forethought and wit to book a taxi through the hotel to meet me. Although going through immigration and customs was smooth, outside the airport there was total chaos. A wall of noise and heat. I had treated myself to a decent hotel on the beach and was not disappointed when I made the final journey from car to check-in desk. The hotel was beautiful. You felt like you were outside inside, if you know what I mean, it was all open. Palm trees and tropical plants everywhere, waterways winding through the gardens leading to the beach. Fountains and waterfalls in the space between the accommodation buildings. Glass lifts on the outside of the hotel floors.

My room had a view towards the bay with a balcony where I could sit and look out for dolphins and birds. I was glad I had brought binoculars because I could spend hours enjoying the local wildlife from my private perch. But first things first, text home to say I had arrived. Text Diana to say I had arrived. Unpack a little, then explore the hotel to get my bearings and have lunch before sitting on the beach. I'll admit to feeling daunted walking alone into a big dining room and decided instead on a light snack at the bar. But the feeling quickly passed because the Mexicans were truly lovely people and so helpful. No need to be shy, the genuine warmth and authenticity that emanated from the big smiles put me right at ease. So I sat down and decided to stuff myself with proper guacamole!

I met up with Diana two days later, she was staying just down the road from me. It was pure joy seeing her beaming face and open arms coming towards me as I walked up the drive to her hotel. We laughed at the craziness of it all, meeting here having not seen each other since the workshop in Maine a year and a half earlier. I met a few of the other participants who had also arrived. The afternoon was spent in continuous flitting between languages, I was pleased with the added bonus of improving my French.

On the Saturday morning, coinciding with my birthday, it was time to pack up and complete the final leg of the journey. The whole group met at the maritime terminal at the harbour where we were met by the boat shuttle. Yes, I was using every form of transport known to man it seemed. The boat was essentially an open metal hull with a massive outboard engine at the back and a canvas covering to provide some shade. I don't know how we did it, but twenty-odd people with luggage managed to squeeze aboard that thing. And then we set off across the bay for a 40-minute wild ride.

I think it was here that I started to feel the joy of letting go again. Just immersing myself in the moment, all senses fired up. The roar of the engine, the wind whipping around my hair and clothes, the bright sun reflecting off the water, the smell of the sea. With every passing minute I left the known further and further behind me. I honestly didn't care about anything. I felt free. Open to possibilities. Ready to meet the unknown…

Which was a good thing, because when we arrived at Xinalani eco-resort, the only way to get onto shore was to hop out of the boat and wade to land. Totally for real. The staff would literally carry our bags on their shoulders from the boat to our rooms. It was like being in a film and entering a magical far-away world. The resort was built into a jungle hillside with all the buildings constructed out of local materials, mostly wood. Every structure faced the sea – the open dining room, the spa, the bungalows and the yoga shalas. The whole place was connected by stairs and bamboo bridges.

As I passed the various rooms on the way to my allocated abode, following my bearer, I noticed that each room had a little saying in a frame, a yogic thought, on the wall by the door. I wondered what would be on mine. I also couldn't help but notice that we were climbing a fair distance from the reception/dining area. How many stairs were there exactly? We finally turned a corner marked by waist-high bright red, pink, blue and purple flowers and there it was, my private jungle bungalow for a week. And what was my mantra sent from the universe, in the frame?

*-The practice of peace and
reconciliation is one of the most
vital and artistic of human actions-*

Wow, okay, well that was relevant given where I was with Hamish. Something to chew on for seven days.

The young man put my suitcase on the floor and I found myself alone and taking in the surroundings. It was hard to believe. Beyond anything I could imagine. Underneath the square raised wooden roof the room had only three whitewashed stone walls, the fourth side of the square being completely open into the jungle and the sea beyond. So, from the bed you looked right out onto the balcony and the lush foliage. The sound of lapping waves against the shoreline was continuous. At night, your only protection from the elements was a canvas curtain that you would unroll from the ceiling to the floor. The ensuite bathroom was also open with a gap between the surrounding wall and roof on two sides. It was beautifully and sympathetically designed to merge the accommodation into the environment. In other words, you *were* the jungle – through your eyes, ears, nose and skin. And yeah, it was hot and humid all right!

My long journey's end was rounded off by a gorgeous dinner where the group gathered properly for the first time. And dear Diana had managed to organise a birthday cake and a bouquet of flowers for me as well, as if she hadn't had enough to do already as retreat leader. I felt safe and welcomed. It was going to be okay.

The next morning I woke up with a sore throat. Oh no, you've got to be kidding me. I hadn't been ill for years and now this, and here of all places. It seemed cruel. Thanks a lot, universe… My normal response would be a rant of self-pity but I actually felt quite calm. This surprised me. I decided to work with acceptance, not resistance, and let this physical process take its course. It was obviously meant to happen and there was nothing I could do about it. Instead, I picked up the spa treatment menu for a good perusal. Diana had told me about a masseuse who worked there called Angel (yes, really) who was phenomenal, and to make sure I booked him specifically. The treatment options were as exotic as the surroundings – the Tequila boost scrub & polish (including a shot of tequila to finish), the Happy Yogi Massage – it was hard to choose. But hey, in for a penny, in for a pound, so I went for it and settled on "Chocolate Obsession". Yes, that's right, I was going to be scrubbed and rubbed with chocolate for 90 minutes. It wasn't a hard sell to be honest:

The cacao seeds' benefits have been revered since prehispanic times because they increase endorphin levels & regulate mood, digestion and sleep. Start with an exquisite scrub and wrap that will prepare your skin for an aromatic chocolate oil massage.
You'll end up with a fierce appetite for life.

What was not to like about that? If that wasn't going to sort me out, nothing would. Angel was available after the first yoga class on Monday morning. A perfect way to start the week.

The rest of the Sunday passed peacefully as I explored the resort and began to relax into the rhythm. First of all, the yoga practice was awesome, exactly what I had hoped for. Diana, working alongside her yoga colleague Linda, taught an authentic, solid Hatha yoga style based on years of experience. Plenty of breaths, cues, adjustments and use of props. It was strong, though, I could feel where I was lacking strength, but at the same time it was like falling into a deep embrace. Being a teacher and rarely a student myself, I felt especially grateful to be at the receiving end.

The main yoga shala added to the deeply spiritual ambience. It sat at the top of the hill looking out to sea. This was a huge square of polished wood floor open on all sides with a high slanting straw roof. It felt like you were actually in the jungle canopy surrounded by lush vegetation. You could see and hear the tropical birds larking in the branches all around you. And speaking of trees, in keeping with the respectful environmental ethos of the resort, the shala had been built around an actual tree, whose trunk rose out of the floor and exited through the roof. Sea breezes wafted through the space to cool you down during and after practice.

The other joyful discovery was the food. Oh my god, the food. We were to live by their adage "you are what you eat". And I did. The offering was traditional Mexican-inspired fare made with mostly local ingredients. The vibrancy of the jungle was reflected on the plate, all your senses tingling with the colour, the aroma and the texture of the recipes. All diets were catered for, gluten free, vegan, dairy free, we could choose whatever we fancied. We could start the day with an optional light snack at 7.00 am but the main breakfast was after the morning yoga class. Followed by lunch, followed by an early dinner after the late afternoon yoga class. It meant you were never more than three hours away from the next meal. Heaven! Finding it hard to exercise on an empty stomach in the morning, I opted for a pre-class cup of cinnamon coffee (that you ladled out into your mug from a beautifully painted ceramic cauldron, oh yeah) and a banana which I savoured from a quiet table looking at the sun's early rays dancing across the bay, the occasional pelican gliding smoothly just feet above the water.

On Monday morning the sore throat had moved up into a significant head cold, I could feel the congestion building up. The only thing worse than a cold is a cold in the heat. Hopefully the chocolate would work some magic, I thought, as I made my way along the bridge to the spa that sat on top of the rocks at the edge of the beach. In the small bamboo lined reception, I presented myself to the waiting Angel. My anxieties were quickly dispelled by his wide welcoming smile and deep brown eyes full of empathy. His voice was like honey, lowering my blood pressure with every reassuring word he uttered. He positively radiated calmness, serenity and peace.

He led me to a little treatment room open to the sea and left me to undress. I stripped bare and laid face down on the table, the soothing surf loud in my ears. I decided to let go, to hand myself over to Angel's care. The scent of the chocolate, first as a scrub and then as oil, was totally intoxicating. I was transported somewhere else, to another plane, as all the tension in my body was smoothed out, painful though it was. I was so tight! But as I slowly softened I could feel the emotions stirring. Oh no, not here, please, don't cry now. Standing in the reception afterwards, hardly able to stand up as I paid, Angel said,

"You need to let go of the fear, Mina, let go of the grief. You're holding here and here," putting his hand on his heart and then on his throat. "You must open up," he added, spreading his arms wide to each side, leaning slightly back on his heels and standing tall. "And look up when you walk, not down. Trust your steps and where you are going."

Okay, this really was more than I could bear. I had not told him anything about myself, my loss, nothing, he had just felt it through my body. The tears were pressing hard now and I couldn't speak. So I just nodded, whispered "thank you so much" and walked as quickly as I could back my bungalow.

What is it with me and the jungle? It was Bali all over again but perhaps more intense this time. There was clearly something about this environment that left me nowhere to hide. The physical challenge of the heat and the humidity combined with some sleep debt seemed to have a profound effect. Not to mention the intense ache in my whole body from going up and down all those stairs. It turned out my bungalow was in between the yoga shala at the top of the hill and the dining room at the bottom. So, every day it was: walk down to early breakfast, climb up to top for yoga, walk down to breakfast, climb up to room to change, walk down to beach, climb up to room to change, climb up to top for yoga, walk down to room to change, walk down to dinner, climb up to room for the night. Then add little extra trips like spa appointment and the time I did some yoga on my own in the shala. I counted it all out and calculated I was going up and down on average 1600 steps a day. No wonder I hurt. And like in the yoga class, I was shocked at my level of unfitness. Well, if nothing else, I was going to have buns of steel by the end of this.

Through the emotional and physical pain, I reflected with irony my thought about not needing to deal with Francesca's death on this trip. That I had "finished the work", or "completed the grieving". That I was "done". The universe had called me out on it and shown me it had other plans. I spent the rest of the day in my room, crying on and off, letting the waves of sadness come and wash over me in rhythm to the lapping waves along the shore below. Francesca was right there, so clear in my mind. My heart ached so badly from the unexpressed and trapped love, my body at times convulsing with the emotional pain as I lay sideways in a foetal position on the bed, clutching a pillow to my chest for comfort. My throat felt tight with the pressure of emotion pushing at it from below. Yet there was relief in the releasing. I didn't resist. I couldn't have even if I had wanted to.

I paused only for a quick lunch before retreating again. Diana caught a glimpse of me in the dining room and came right over having sensed the state of affairs.

"Oh my god, Mina, are you okay?"

"Yeah, I saw Angel this morning. You sure were right about him."

"Oh, okay, I understand. You've obviously got stuff going on. Well, you just take whatever time you need and come see me if you need to talk, yeah?"

"Yeah. I don't think I can manage yoga this afternoon."

"No problem, sweetie. Do what you need to do."

It was at that lunch I felt the beginning of another shift within myself. I looked around the room and the people there. Once again, I was where I needed to be, far away from home with a loving supportive group. There was no judgement here, only acceptance and understanding. I had picked up a few stories and realised everyone had stuff. These were life survivors. Survived cancer, survived bereavement, survived divorce, survived dramatic career changes and other life-changing events. These women *knew*, they *got it*. I felt truly safe, held, contained and looked after. Deeply nourished. The group, the yoga, the sea, the food – together they made up Team Mina. I could lean in with all my might, the team would hold, it could take whatever I threw at it. I made myself a promise to let the emotions come whenever I needed to for the rest of the week. And to let it go.

I had been dealing with these waves of grief throughout the week but rode them bravely, my tears mixing with the copious mucous I blew out of my nose from the head cold. One day I was resting in the shade by the beach when I felt another one come. Right, I thought, let's really do this, let's get this out. I got off the lounger and walked to the water's edge by a private spot, wading up to my knees. With my feet firmly planted in the sand, I put a hand on each knee and bent over, torso parallel to the water, looking down. I just let the tears and the snot drop into the Pacific, emptying my head quite literally of, well, everything. I don't know how long I stood there but it felt incredibly cleansing. And grounding. At some point it was enough and I walked back to the shade.

Then one afternoon came the rain. Jungle rain. Yeah, remember that? The sky suddenly darkened and the heavens opened. I was in my bungalow at the time, sitting on my bed and looking right at it through the open space towards the balcony. But I was in a different place within myself now. Rather than feel like sheltering and retreating from it, I felt strangely drawn towards it. I got up, stepped out onto the balcony and stood there. Within minutes I was soaked through. Unlike Bali, this time the weighty water drops felt liberating. The rain wasn't my enemy, it was my friend. Relaxing my shoulders and turning my face up towards the sky, I let Mother Nature wash me clean of heavy emotions, of my past. Like a child being bathed by a loving parent, I felt soothed and light. When I had had enough, I walked back under the roof and changed my clothes.

Halfway through the week I had found myself in deep conversation with one of the ladies, herself going through a massive life shift. It was a spontaneous meeting of hearts and minds. She reminded me of the futility in falling into our stories, in having regrets. We make our choices, there is no one to blame. I loved her warmth and her energy so it felt right to tell her about Francesca. It was good to verbalise it (and probably unblocking my throat energetically), to hear myself say her name out loud. I rarely ever hear her name. It sounds so silly but it's very important. I shouldn't be afraid to bring Francesca into the light, into the now, after all. She doesn't live in the shadows, she is everywhere. In any case, this woman's spiritual gift to me was her insight that *"each moment prepares you for the next moment"*. Indeed.

Diana had been my anchor too. By the end of the week we had had two deep and frank conversations, because sometimes you just have to be *told*, you know? In brutal terms, by someone you trust and who loves you. I had been writing a journal since I arrived and penned what had been said:

Conversation no 1: I have to get over myself! I must accept that Hamish is never going to give me what I think I need. He is not going to fill whatever hole I have in me. The reality is that no one is. I have to deal with that hole myself. I need to let go of the longing, the yearning. This is what is driving the frustration, the unhappiness. "It's killing you," she said, pointing to my chest.

Conversation no 2: I permeate anger and resentment. I am very self-contained, I contain it all, but to contain it from others I am naturally aloof, I separate myself. This protective containing protects myself from hurt and pain and others from my anger but by definition creates a shell that makes me hard. I keep banging my head against this hardness, creating resistance. I need to SOFTEN and open up my heart.

That's what tough love sounds like and I needed it. She was absolutely right. We later laughed about it, me describing it as her taking a machete to my coconut-like heart and cracking it open. Because it needed to open up more and it just wasn't going to open up any other way. I reflected again on Eckhart Tolle's advice that instead of resisting, let things flow *through you*. If nothing flows through, in or out, I would always be in a downward spiral of depletion, with anger and resentment accumulating. Hamish gave me the freedom to do what I needed to do, go where I needed to go. He was an enabler, not a barrier. It was a moment of clarity – it wasn't about Hamish at all, it was about my broken, hardened heart.

Before I knew it the last day arrived. I felt cleansed, transformed and unburdened in every way. I felt lightness for the first time in my life. The energy of the whole group had in fact shifted. I wasn't the only one who had had an uplifting massage from Angel and/or unpacked some shit to leave behind. There was a collective vibrancy, a relief. And love. As a special surprise after the final dinner, which was a beautiful buffet laid out next to the pool on the beach front lit only by candles, Diana had organised a salsa dancer to entertain us. It turned out to be a dance lesson. So there we were in lines next to the bar, trying to follow this amazing guy doing the salsa steps to loud South American music. The idea was we would learn the steps of a sequence, then pair up and each pair would dance the sequence to the group. Yes, another opportunity to let go, I thought.

I somehow found myself paired up with the husband of one of the women, with her approval of course. He and I learned the steps okay and our moment to step into the limelight arrived. There was no time to hesitate as the dance teacher cued in the beat for us to begin. Off we went, swept by the music and laughter. It was pure joy, everyone clapping and smiling. As I swung my arms out from side to side in one of the moves, opening up my chest fully, I felt something lifting. Something loosened.

The next morning, sitting in the dining room with my packed suitcase waiting for the boat shuttle, I felt ready to leave the jungle and go home. It was time. During the week British Airways had suddenly cancelled my return flight through Phoenix so I had been rerouted through Dallas Fort Worth. I'd fly there and pick up the overnight flight to London, doing the return in one go. As the plane thundered down the Puerto Vallarta Airport runway I felt like my spirits alone could lift that thing off the ground and fly me all the way back.

Then something strange happened not long into the flight. I had settled down with my drink (tomato juice with spices, always the same when flying) and was enjoying the air conditioning when suddenly in my mind's eye I was transported back to Francesca's last moments in that bedroom. I could feel us huddling close around her, I could hear her rasping breath slowing, slowing, slowing down. Physically I felt my chest tighten, I couldn't breathe. Rather than panic and force myself out of the reverie, I decided to stay there and re-live it. Yeah, let's just go there. I placed the tips of the index finger and middle finger of my right hand right in the middle of my chest, between my breasts where the heart chakra is. I noticed this place was sore already. I pressed really hard, shaking the fingers slightly as if to loosen the painful knot that was there. Free it up so I could breathe. I stayed with her dying moments, breathing deeply, in out, in out, kneading my fingers into the heart chakra. The tears flowed quietly down my cheeks.

I have to say that at this point I was just so grateful for our totally disconnected modern life. The guy next to me and the people across the aisle were all engrossed with their mobile phones and tablets, headphones stuffed deeply into their ears. I think I was the only person not looking at a digital device. And the stewardess was busy with her work, trying to get through service as quickly as possible with minimal interaction. If she could have tossed the bags of nuts into our laps at walking pace, she would have. It was comical in a way. I was having this profound experience and nobody noticed, they were oblivious to their surroundings. It was great. I actually felt supported, their complete detachment oddly comforting. I don't know how long I stayed this way, it was probably a few minutes but seemed like hours. I breathed through Francesca's dying breath and hovered over her lifeless body once more. Then it was over and I came to. I lowered my right hand and just rested for a while. I felt quite peaceful and calm. Whatever that was, it was significant. I had survived it and come out the other side. Perhaps flying through the ether had something to do with it, hovering literally in space, closer to the cosmos. I spent the rest of the flight to Dallas writing a new yoga sequence for the class based on all the yoga learning I had gleaned from Diana and Linda.

Energy is not bound by time and space, rather it is like an invisible fascia that envelops the world and everything in it all the time. So a shift in energy in one place can be sensed in another place at the same time. I learned this as I walked into the house, finally arriving after the long journey. I left my suitcase standing just inside the door and plonked myself down on the floor to greet a very excited Barley. Hamish perched on a step at the bottom of the stairs. Through tears and tiredness I shared the headlines of the experience. I apologised for channelling anger and frustration at him. I mean, all the awful things that had happened to me – divorce, Francesca's illness and death, and my life preceding those events – had nothing to do with him and his Asperger's. It wasn't his fault. That was my stuff.

He seemed relieved, but I also sensed a lightness in him that hadn't been there when I had left. This became quite apparent as he invited me to have a look at what he'd been up to while I was away. I followed him into the kitchen where I was presented with a large (intimidating) new coffee machine, the sort with bean grinder, tamper, and milk frother all in one. He was now an official self-taught barista. Then on to the utility room where there was an ice cream/sorbet machine sitting on the counter. Back to the kitchen for a taster spoonful of his homemade vanilla ice cream. But that was not all. Wouldn't I like to go into the downstairs loo for a moment? I walked in to discover he had redecorated the whole bathroom, right down to the details. Gone was the harsh cold white paint on the walls, ceiling and door, replaced with warm glowing peach hues. There was a new soap dish next to the basin with matching Molton Brown hand wash and hand cream in it, a decorative shell placed in the middle. On the other side of the basin was a glass container with lemon scent sticks. On the window sill was a candle and a little statuette of a whale tail, sticking up as if diving into the wood surface. It was amazing, I was quite overwhelmed.

So, as I was unburdening myself in Mexico, he was being freed up at home. An energy shift had taken place that had created space for lightness and creativity. This shift held right through Christmas, which was the best Christmas in a very long time for me. Karina came to stay from Bristol and

187

Malcolm joined us. It felt like a proper festive family celebration.

You were never born; you will never die.
You have never changed; you can never change.
Unborn, eternal, immutable, immemorial, you do
not die when the body dies.
Bhagavad Gita 2.20

Chapter 10: Not for the last time

Was that the end of my spiritual quest? Did I sail happily into the spiritual sunset?

Not quite. The universe had more to offer me as it always does. In March 2020 it served up Covid-19, which literally "went viral" transcending all boundaries and causing a national lockdown.

As it happened, Hamish and I both fell ill with it at the beginning of that month but fortunately were able to manage recovery without medical intervention. It took several weeks to get back to normal energy levels though. By then I was enveloped in a beautiful stillness. The world had gone quiet. There was nowhere to go, nothing to chase, no reason to grasp. This sky was so blue, the animal life so abundant, the colours so bright. I hadn't known a spring like it. Every dog walk was an opportunity to just breathe it all in, to just be.

Having resisted at first, I put my yoga classes online and discovered a whole new way of teaching.

And in the stillness was a constant invitation to reflect on my situation and where I'd arrived. I accepted that invitation. Why had I attracted Hamish and the Asperger's into my life? What was it about running into this recurring theme of lacking, of disappointment, of being left wanting? Well, living in Covid isolation with Asperger's on my own with no access to the balancing forces of family and friends (except the dog) left me nowhere to hide. The purpose was to face *myself* surely. Because the AS-NT partnership dynamic remained challenging. Whenever my *samskara* was triggered and feelings of anger, bitterness, resentment, frustration, disappointment, sadness, self-pity, etc. surfaced, they were returned in their entirety. Nothing was soothed or made okay, which is the way of Asperger's – remember, it's a case of *can't* not *won't*. Sounds exhausting? It was. My head was just getting more and more sore banging against his "wall".

I had a choice. I could keep banging my head or just… stop. Yeah, that's right, just stop. How about taking all my spiritual yogic knowledge and experience and applying it properly this time. What did that mean? Letting go of all my baggage. The anger, the resentment, *all of it*. The reason why some feeling of stuckness remained was because I was still clinging onto my expectations (that he would change and I would have a "normal" relationship among other things) which were never going to happen. I also realised that only someone

190

with Asperger's could manage that process as I battled with myself. He was immovable. My expectations were not going to be met, end of story. I just had to lay it all down and leave it. I needed to get out of my head, my intellect, and into my *heart*. To stop being ruled by my mind, my Ego and my past.

I saw it now. I was at the centre of my storm, I was generating my pain and suffering. Joy, love, fulfilment, contentment, all those good things weren't *out there*, in someone else or job role or fancy house. They were *in here*, in me. Because I was also the creator of my own joy and love. That being the case, it would therefore follow that I could make that hole, the emptiness, vanish.

It made sense to me. I mean, when I really thought about it, hadn't the universe always given me what I needed and asked for?

When I needed stability and the experience of my own family I met Malcolm.
When I needed guidance with grief and starting my spiritual quest I met Colin.
When I needed to start opening up my heart and trust feminine love I met Joanna.
When I needed to open up my heart a little more I found a dog breeder who matched me with Barley.
When I needed to find the mat and my calling as a yoga teacher I met Debs.
When I needed to step up my spiritual game and have support with Asperger's I met Sarah.
When I needed more support in developing my yoga and letting go of more stuff I met Diana.

Each special person had a heart opening effect that helped me heal. Because it wasn't just about the pain from losing Francesca, it was about healing myself completely from my *whole past* and be free of my *samskara* once and for all. So, how could it be that Hamish did not also have a healing purpose for me? That he was another key offering from the universe? In fact, the universe had made sure he was in place *before* the "After Francesca" journey had even begun. Yes, I could see how his piece fitted neatly into the puzzle.

Lockdown lifted and I ended up having the most extraordinary summer ever. In September the year before, I had booked a special 2 ½ week mother-daughter trip to my native Norway. It was something we had talked about for a while. I had planned it very carefully. As is often the case, you tend to feel more curious about foreign lands than your own country. I grew up in Oslo but had never seen Norway properly, fully. So the idea of the trip was to reconnect Karina and I with our roots, and also to fulfil her wish to show me the glaciers she had studied for her university geography dissertation (she had gone to Norway seven years before, to the Jostedal ice sheet, to collect her own data). We were to start our adventure above the Arctic Circle, in Tromsø, and work our way down to Bergen by boat, plane and rental car, taking in the glaciers en route. When all the Covid quarantines were put in place around Europe the trip was in jeopardy. Would I have to cancel it all, the thought of which was very upsetting? Better leave it to the universe to decide then. I left all the bookings in place.

One week before we were due to fly, the quarantines in the UK and Norway were lifted. We could go! And we had the trip of a lifetime. On our return, there was a question mark over another holiday booking, this time a family trip to the Lake District at the end of August. Would we have to cancel due to Covid? Again, we were lucky and I spent a magical two weeks in more glorious northern scenery filled with dog walks and stunning views. I felt more grounded, grateful and content than I had in a long time. My body was at peak fitness, I glowed from top to toe.

And then the unthinkable happened. I had a horrible accident and broke my arm. Yes, that's right, I properly shattered it.

Two weeks after I got home from the Lake District I was riding Joanna's horse (I rode in my younger days and when I got the offer at the beginning of summer to exercise her horse I thought it would be fun and add to my fitness) and lost my balance. The horse hadn't done anything, I was simply slowing him down in a light canter to put my foot back in the stirrup when I slid out of the saddle in the corner of the indoor riding school… and into a cement wall at considerable speed, leading with the left side of my body. I had just enough time to think "Oh no!" then BOOM! I was on the floor leaning back against the wall, my left arm flopped grotesquely by my side. I knew it was broken and I knew it was bad.

Then something strange happened. I was overwhelmed with gratitude and joy. I became euphoric. I just kept repeating in my mind and out loud "thank you, thank you, thank you." I was alive. It was just my arm. I was still breathing and thinking. I could tell the rest of me was okay. And even as the most intense pain I have ever experienced in my life set in, I just felt so grateful. This had been a really close shave. I was going to see the orthopaedic doctors, not the neurologists. I could walk out of the building and get into the car with Hamish who came to collect me and drive me to A&E. I shouted and screamed in agony the whole way, mind, but I was compos mentis and fully aware.

I was right, it was bad. The x-ray showed multiple fractures of the humerus bone (technical term comminuted fracture) including a really nasty diagonal snap and partial shoulder dislocation. I'll spare you the details but I ended that day being driven home by Hamish with my arm in nothing but a sling, having been told gravity was going to align the bone back together. Seriously? That's it? Yes, I had heard that correctly through the fog of pain and morphine (which only took the edge off slightly). I don't know how I got through that first night. But I spent the next month sleeping upright in a sitting position and getting through each day hour by hour.

Now I was faced with "the choice". Again.

Option 1: fall into self-pity, "why me?", "why me *again*?", "why me again *now*, when everything was going so well?", "nothing good ever lasts" plus anger, despair, resentment - straight into my familiar always-waiting-for-me *samskara*. Because it would fit so neatly on the list of "Sad and Terrible Things That Happen to Poor Mina", wouldn't it?

Option 2: put it on the ever-growing list of "Good Things That Happen to Mina" instead. Surrender and trust and find the learning opportunity.

Sure, I could just put it down to bad luck, to one-of-those-things, to "shit happens". Or I could look inwards at what was left of the baggage to be shifted. I did both but landed on the right side. You bet I had days of anger, despair and resentment, the pain saw to that. I hated the loss of control, the vulnerability and the helplessness. I was trapped in neediness. All the very things I had tried to avoid to protect myself, to protect my heart. The very things I had disliked seeing in others. Talk about facing yourself!

So here's the thing. Ever since the day that I realised Hamish had Asperger's two years before, and in spite of the Covid induced personal growth opportunity as I've described, I had harboured a particularly negative and self-destructive thought. A thought in the back of my mind that over time had gathered quite a lot of energy and momentum: "Nothing had better happen to me because there will be no one to look after me." That is what low-level, lurking-in-the-background, seething resentment sounds like by the way. And so here I was, in the very situation I feared the most because I had energetically created it. You could go as far as to say my negative energy and expectation, my fear, threw me into that wall.

Either way, this particular "growth opportunity" began with Hamish cutting me out of my riding clothes with scissors that night back from A & E and carefully wiping me down with a warm wet flannel to get rid of the smell of horse, stable and sweat while I stood naked on the bathroom floor. He built a stack of pillows on the bed to support my upright sleeping posture. For the next few weeks he helped me bathe, wash my hair, cut up my food, put my hair in a ponytail, get dressed. He did the dog walking and the food shopping. I wasn't going to be driving for some time. Malcolm kept us fed, voluntarily stepping into the role of Personal Dinner Chef. Other amazing, kind friends offered help with dog walking and giving me lifts. And thanks to all the digital tools, I could lean into supportive video calls with caring people who weren't local.

And the arm? Unbelievably, gravity did do its thing and pulled the broken bits of bone together back into alignment. Two months later and the arm was pretty near fully straight and back to its unswollen normal size. Between my yoga practice – the most awesome physical healing tool in the world – and the physiotherapy, my range of movement improved day by day. This arm and shoulder would fully heal given time and love. I returned to online teaching and the good wishes from students helped me more than they will ever know.

On the back of this "story of a broken arm", I have permanently fired my "No, I'll do it myself", "No, I can manage," "No, I don't need help" Ego self. Instead I say a big "Yes" to it all! That's right, I accepted help and it didn't hurt one bit, fancy that. Being needy didn't kill me. In fact, it felt good to be helped, to feel how supported I really was if I stopped doubting. That awful, self-destructive voice of the abandoned child crying "it's not about me, it's never about me..." that had been ringing in my ears since childhood has finally been extinguished. She is comforted at last. It took Francesca and her early departure, the subsequent pain and suffering, the thousands of miles flown around the world and all the lovely people I have met (and rediscovered) along the way, not to mention a shattered humerus bone, to get here. Because only when I was physically incapacitated and my life came to a grinding halt, when the universe had my full and undivided attention, could I run the ultimate experiment called "what happens if something bad happens to Mina?" The answer is: love. And with the love I have found joy and gratitude.

Breaking my arm made it all about me. It was the only way I could see what was there all along but didn't really believe. It was the only way I could get out of my *samskara*, out of my self-created, self-limiting ditch, and climb over the edge to see the full wonder that is life. *My life.* I am not abandoned or alone. I knew there was love, of course I did, but I had never dared to fully trust it.

I felt like the universe was saying to me, "Do you get it now? Do you finally get it now? Can you take surrender-and-trust into your very Being and keep it there? Live by it every single day no matter what?" Because it's as simple as that. You can read as many books as you like and discuss spirituality until the cows come home, but it's not until the heart is completely open that you will truly feel it, truly "get it". To *know* it to the core of your very being.

The second lockdown in the UK offered another opportunity to take stock and reflect. I chose to surrender and trust that:

- I would receive what I need when I need it in whatever form it appears: a person I meet, a work opportunity or an unforeseen event.
- The universe has my back, all I have to do is follow the trail it lays out for me.
- I therefore don't need to worry about the future and control the outcome in any detail.

What else have I learned that I think is important to share? Here are some key points:

"Soulmate" is a myth
Out on a dog walk with Sarah a while back, we started talking about this popular idea of "soulmate". I have never liked this word because it implies that only one person can "mate with your soul" as it were, that only one person can truly know you and connect with you on a deep level. Can really *see* you. And that this person has to be your

partner/spouse. This romanticised notion of soulmate is a myth, frankly. This is especially true in the Western culture where the focus is finding your one true love, the person who is going to meet all your needs forever. How many films and TV programmes have you seen, how many books have you read, that present this same story? Oh, the pressure to find him/her! And the despair and disappointment that comes when the search bears no fruit. You can't find that person, or the person you thought was "it", isn't…

What did Sarah think?

"It's a myth, I agree," she said. "You can have many soulmates. Your partner, of course, but also close friends and family. Everyone in your life is a soulmate because everyone you meet can teach you something even if that thing is painful."

I hadn't thought of it like that. This made more sense. We can attach to more than one person in a lifetime and each one of them bears gifts. Gifts that help you figure out who you are and shape you into a better you. A shoulder to cry on. An ear to listen to your story and your thoughts. Wisdom from their life experience. Useful advice. Laughter. Shared joy. Reassurance. Rejection. Disappointment. They hold up a mirror in different ways so you can see yourself from different angles. Even people who hurt you are teaching you because they show you the contrast. You appreciate the light more if you have spent quality time in the dark, don't you?

Now, there are examples of where two people can be exclusive soulmates for each other, don't get me wrong. I know some couples like this, and it's beautiful to see. But it should not be an expectation or a goal. If it happens naturally, organically, then of course that is lovely. What the universe has shown me, though, is an alternative point of view. It was explained to me by someone I met recently. She offered me a reworked version of Sleeping Beauty. We all know the fairy tale story: the princess is in the tower asleep waiting for "the one" to kiss and awaken her. The handsome Prince Charming fights his way through the brambles and thorns to reach her and they live happily ever after. Well, instead of us interpreting that literally and looking externally for that someone in the form of a physical partner, how about if what we are looking for is inside ourselves? Not the one, but the One? As in the Source, the universe? We could turn our attention inward, fighting through the thorny brambles of our stuff, our past, our story and the negative thoughts that block us and awaken *ourselves*. Balance our own male (the prince) and female (the princess) energies, unifying the two principles. Open up our own heart. Yes, I like that version, I like it very much. That makes more sense as a story.

It starts with you.

Only you can change yourself, can heal yourself. No one else can do it for you. I'm sure we'd love to outsource this rather than take responsibility, and we do it by projecting our needs and our shit into others. It's so much easier if someone else carries your burden rather than own it yourself, right? I think we have all tried this at some point. Working with blame. It's always someone else's fault. This may work for a time but ultimately fails. The pain, unease, unhappiness and dissatisfaction remain, you can't shake them.

It's more effort but the way forward is self-care, self-love. I know, I know, this is an oft-used cliché you see and hear everywhere but it's true. You will arrive here when you have run away from yourself for however long and discovered you still can't hide. And then you discover how much better it feels to be kind to yourself, even just a little bit. It can start with anything from treating yourself to a massage or going out for a meal, to something bigger like leaving an unfulfilling job or ditching an unsupportive partner. The more you love yourself, the more confident you will become and open to things that are of real benefit to you.

Don't wait for your life to begin.

Start now. Today. This moment. Drop your story, climb out of your *samskara* and get over yourself. If you don't deal with your stuff, it will keep coming back at you until you do. Have you noticed this? Perhaps it's a pattern of meeting inappropriate partners, or butting your head up against unhelpful bosses or colleagues at work, or the jobs themselves keep leading to dead ends, or making what turns out to be the wrong type of friends. It's when you get the thought "I've been here before", when a bad or unhelpful situation feels familiar. Yeah, that's right, you're still in your *samskara* and the universe is nudging you to get out. To quote Stephen Cope, "what we resist, persists".

I highly recommend doing something challenging, something out of the daily routine and away from home to kick-start the healing process. For me, I discovered that travelling solo to foreign cultures, to Bali and Mexico, was super helpful in this regard. To hang out there all alone and see what happens with no agenda. To face my fears. These trips really helped me connect to, and believe in, ever-present human love and kindness.

Sometimes what you want is not what you need.
You are not your Ego so you don't need to listen to what it's telling you. The Ego controls you through fear. Still not sure about that? Still clinging on to that wheel of karma, going around and around in circles attached to the results? Then look around you at the animals and plants in nature. So beautiful, so serene, so *knowing*. They fulfil their life's purpose effortlessly because they are simply *being*. They have no Ego. We can be the same, we don't need it either.

It took me a while to get this, but I can now see how true this is. I wanted the cosy family unit: husband and children with me as stay-at-home mother forever. No, that didn't happen. I didn't want Francesca to die. Sorry, no, she died. I wanted a female dog. No, you don't. I wanted the fairy tale marriage the second time. Nope, wrong again. I thought counselling was my calling. Actually no, it's just a step along the way.

For a long time I thought the universe was just one big "NO" obviously. I just kept on being punished, over and over. But if you turn it around and see these things as growth opportunities, as landmarks on the map of your life that you can navigate by, suddenly it feels like a "YES" instead. In any given moment you are where you need to be, and with whoever you need to be with. Some years ago I heard Oprah Winfrey say, "there is no such thing as failure, you're simply going in the wrong direction". Well, that's a very different way of looking at life, isn't it? More positive, more supportive and reassuring. Wish I had understood that properly when I left university. Life cannot be *against* you, it is always *for* you. You're just looking at it the wrong way around.

The last thing to open up is the heart.

After your head and body. Of course it is. It's where we are most vulnerable, especially if you've been hurt. All I can say is that that was my journey, my heart was the last stop. It had to happen in that order because I couldn't go near it at the beginning, like a post-operative wound that is so sensitive and painful you can't bear anyone touching it. But then gradually it heals and it's okay to go there, the stitches come out and it doesn't hurt as much. It can tolerate a bit of pressure on it. Over time all that is left is the scar that indicates something happened but you have recovered.

That's why it feels safer to stay in the head and run your life through logic, analysing, intellectualising and rationalising. Our emotions then get stored in the body, which perhaps becomes shut down too. Eventually there is no body awareness, your head is disconnected from the rest of you. At some point you only become aware of your body when it starts to hurt somewhere. Then you have to choose between dealing with that pain and finding out what the real cause is or ignoring it through distraction (like work) and/or drugs and/or alcohol and so on.

The good news is that you can start to open whatever has been closed at any time. Open the mind, open the body, open the heart. And yoga lovingly holds your hand the whole way. You see, when your heart breaks, it ultimately breaks *open*.

Work with gratitude…

…as often and as much as you can. I have discovered how important this is. Having a *samskara* that kept me in anger and resentment meant I always saw the glass half empty. I had resigned myself to being an eternal pessimist, that that was just how I was, that was my lot. My attention therefore rested constantly on what there wasn't rather than what there was. On what I wasn't getting. This is particularly easy to do when you are in a relationship with an Asperger's person. In actual fact, Hamish was giving me something very important. Freedom. Freedom to pursue career options. Freedom to get a dog and share the care. Freedom to fly to Bali, to Mexico, or anywhere else for that matter, to do whatever I needed to do there. Freedom to remain friends with my first husband. These are significant gifts. Without him I could not have gone into my self-discovery in such depth. And written this book!

Life is short. Francesca showed me the truth in this popular adage. As I have experienced more than once, your life can turn on a penny, can change in a single moment. So, be grateful and avoid not realising what you have until it's gone. Oh yeah, and remember to choose joy!

Surrender and trust.

This is now my mantra. I chant it to myself during meditation, during *savasana*, during quiet moments when I'm on my own like in the car driving or walking the dog or knitting. It's a continuous comforting reminder to let go. To know fear is a barrier to a fulfilled life. To trust that the universe has got your back. I don't worry about what may or may not happen next. If I'm heading in the wrong direction, it will let me know soon enough.

Nothing is so bad that good cannot come from it.

When something terrible happens, we have two options: fall deeper into our *samskara* or turn adversity into a learning opportunity.

I could easily have chosen to throw myself into my work and pursue my corporate career after Francesca died in order to distract myself from my spiritual dilemma. I could have rushed into another counselling job when I was made redundant. I could have left my marriage immediately when discovering the Asperger's and focused on finding "Mr Right". I am not a victim. We have choices even when we think we don't. Sarah keeps saying to me "choose joy!" and she is right. So, I have discovered that life works out better in the long run with less "this didn't work out, so I'm off" and more "wait a minute, why has it turned out like this, turned out differently to what I expected?"

Therefore, what seems like a loss is actually a gain. I borrow Eknath Easwaran's words here:

Through pain, we learn there is no event, however tragic, from which we cannot learn and grow.

Even when your child dies.

This book is about empowerment. The healing practice of yoga and all the literature behind it is about empowerment. You take the hard knocks when they come and use them to connect to and strengthen your inner Self. This is what I channel through my yoga teaching, encouraging people to tune into the body, find what is being held there and let it go. I say this with complete conviction and sincerity because through pain, perseverance and yoga I have empowered myself. It started with the loss of Francesca which propelled me into gaining more than I could ever have imagined or dreamt of. Her life and early parting was, in this sense, her gift to me. A gift of love and joy.

I'm so glad I was brave enough to embark on the journey and in so doing thank her. I still miss her and think about her every day, but she was right, nothing is for the last time. As the *Bhagavad Gita* explains, we come from the universe, we are of the universe and we return to the universe. It is up to us how we spend the time while we are here, and I hope this story inspires you to empower yourself, to be courageous and take risks. To come out of your self-generated *samskara* and discover that there is more, so much more. And it's all right here, in you. Today.

From the heart with love,

Mina

Photo: Hamish Cameron

**Francesca Eugenie
Blair-Robinson**

**7 October 1995 –
27 November 2007**

**Yoga Teacher Graduation Day
Ubud, Bali 22 April 2017**

Acknowledgements

This was the easiest part of the book to write, conveying heartfelt gratitude to the people who made it possible:

Thank you to Malcolm for giving me two gorgeous girls and for remaining friends and parenting partner. And your nourishing meals during my arm healing of course!

Thank you to Colin for giving me my intellectual confidence and opening up my eyes to the spiritual world. I shall always remember our "coffee and cats" meetings with fondness. Thank you for giving me permission to publish our correspondence.

Thank you to Joanna for being you and for, well, listening. Yeah, just listening, allowing me to feel *heard*. And really *seeing* me when I couldn't see a thing.

Thank you to Barley for your patience hanging in there with me and teaching me how to trust. Also, for connecting me to laughter, playfulness and lightness again.

Thank you to Debs for giving me the gift of yoga which completely transformed my life and steered me in the direction of my calling.

Thank you to the Akasha Yoga Academy training team who held me when I was at my most vulnerable and helped me discover my inner teacher.

Thank you to Sarah for your wisdom and for sharing your healing powers. Through you I learned to really trust the universe. Thank you also for helping me believe in this book.

Thank you to Diana for seeing there was more letting go to do, being honest to call me out on it and providing a safe space for me to do it. And for sharing your yoga teacher knowledge.

Thank you to Hamish for providing me with a life and opportunity that has enabled such intense and profound personal growth. That enabled me to find out who I really am.

Thank you to my lovely daughter Karina who also endured the pain of loss but through her own courage emerged on the other side. Being your mother is the greatest joy.

There are others who played their part along the way, I am grateful to all of you.

And finally thank you dear Francesca, for coming into this world and teaching me, indeed all of us, so much.

Mina's reading

Here is a list of the texts I refer to in the book and/or have influenced me, in case you want to follow up on any of them:

Dr Elisabeth Kubler-Ross, *On Children and Death*
J Philip Newell, *The Book of Creation*
J Philip Newell, *Celtic Benediction*
Kenneth White, *The Bird Path*
Dermot Moran, *The Philosophy of Scottus Eriugena*
Margaret Miles, *Plotinus on Body and Beauty*
John Habgood, *The Concept of Nature*
Stanford Encyclopedia of Philosophy, Heidegger's Aesthetics Online

The Monks of New Skete, *The Art of Raising a Puppy*

BKS Iyengar, *The Path to Holistic Health*
Ray Long, *The Key Poses of Yoga*
Swami Muktibodhananda, *Hatha Yoga Pradipika*
Leslie Kaminoff & Amy Matthews, *Yoga Anatomy*

Stephen Cope, *Yoga and the Quest for the True Self*
Paramahansa Yogananda, *Autobiography of a Yogi*
Eknath Easwaran, *The Essence of The Bhagavad Gita*
Eknath Easwaran, *The Bhagavad Gita*
Alan Watts, *The Wisdom of Insecurity*
Alan Watts, *The Way of Zen*
Wendy Teasdill, *Walking to the Mountain*

The Cloud of Unknowing and other works translated by Clifton Wolters

The Collected Works of St John of the Cross translated by Kieran Kavanaugh and Otilio Rodriguez

Swami Chidvilasananda, *My Lord Loves a Pure Heart*

Swami Chidvilasananda, *The Yoga of Discipline*

Osho, *Living Dangerously*

Caroline Myss, *The Anatomy of the Spirit*

Alan Shearer, *Patanjali's Yoga Sutras*

Georg Feuerstein, *The Yoga Tradition*

James Mallinson, *The Shiva Samhita*

James Mallinson, *The Gheranda Samhita*

Swami Satchidananda, *The Yoga Sutras of Patanjali*

Sadhguru, *Inner Engineering*

Eckhart Tolle, *The Power of Now*

Tony Attwood, *The Complete Guide to Asperger's Syndrome*

Genevieve Edmonds and Dean Worton, *The Asperger Personal Guide*

Printed in Great Britain
by Amazon